GRIEF IS LOVE

MARY DEAL

FOREWORD

I remember hearing the delivery truck backing up with its accompanying repetitive *ding*, alarming others that a vehicle was in reverse. How dare it make a delivery at this time! My mother had just died, and although my world had immediately stopped, the rest of the world continued! How dare it! No moment of silence, no pause; nurses were coming in and out the room. I even heard unrelated laughter outside the room.

Nothing stops us in our tracks quicker than the death of a loved one. And nothing seems to wish to keep us there as unaddressed Grief.

Embracing the pain of our loss can merely be perceived as a pragmatic exercise to remove us from the acute emotional pain we are experiencing, but it is much more than a mere utilitarian exercise. Sitting with our pain sheds light on our love, on what is important and essential in life, and, in short, brings to us a new perspective of our pain and of our emotional suffering.

I met Mary as Ron was dying. I was her Chaplain.

We sat outside at a table and Mary shared with me her and Ron's story. There is power in the Narrative that we have constructed throughout our lives. Our Story is about who we are, what we have done, where we have been, and what hopes we have, or had.

Mary shared with me her and Ron's story—the things they had done, the places they had been, and the various places they had lived while in Hawaii. Mary's story was imbued with meaning, joy, fulfilment, and now it had become shadowed by pain.

I encouraged Mary to speak her love to Ron, but also to begin writing letters to Ron. Mary is an author, an artist, and deeply spiritual. She had no difficulty picking up the pen and to start processing her pain. To the letters were added meaningful poems reflective of her love for Ron, as well as of her pain in his death.

Mary's poems evolved along with her pain. Dark ones began to be mixed with elements of light and joy upon recalling previous times in which things were different.

Grief never really ends. It just becomes different. Processing the pain of our loss through embracing it, writing about it, sitting with it, and asking questions of it, helps to change our perspective of our suffering and pain. Mary recognized that things never *get better* after the loss of a loved one, but they will and do become *different*, and that writing about her pain and embracing such pain was essential in bringing about that difference—a *difference* that allows us new perspectives . . . and even new opportunities.

I have read the poems in this book. Mary usually shared them with me upon their completion. Before you are the very poems that helped Mary gain insight

to her love for Ron, as well as to help her gain insight
into living.

"Tim" ~ M.Div.
Chaplain
Bereavement Counselor
Scottsdale, Arizona

INTRODUCTION

One thing is certain: *Grief Is Love.* When we mourn our dearly departed, we long to hold them again, kiss and hug and continue with life, but we cannot. We're left with no outlet for the love we feel for them, except to hold that very love in our hearts. Facing that they are gone, being unable to express that emotion to them, causes grief. *Grief is love.*

This book is both a tribute to Ronald Jerome Holte, my partner of thirty-one years, and it's a memoir meant to offer aid and encouragement to survivors who endure their own period of grief.

I must warn you that some of the writings included here are sad and heart-wrenching while others may simply be emotionally raw. I am baring my heart. If I can't do that, then what is there with which you who suffer and seek support might find rapport and validation for your own grief and nearly unnatural experiences? As I am learning, grief is not something anyone should have to do alone. The creation of this book comes from a place of pain. Most books I've read dealing with grief and bereavement are written, perhaps a year or more after the author has developed a better grip on their own anguish. Yet, the writing seemed sterile and formal, at least to me. I write this book from inside my pain, while it is ongoing and, at times, maddening.

One thing I ask is that you not feel sorrow for me. While I am normally quiet, meditative, positive, even passive-aggressive, I am *never* the narcissist. I write this book to give insight into the moments of acute anguish and desolation to which you may relate from your own place of distress and find validation for your heartache. Almost everyone in their lifetime will face a period such as this. Some will move through it well. Others, like myself, will have great difficulty enduring it. I bare my soul that others will find validation for their immeasurable sorrows.

If you are squeamish about emotional instability, the process of dying, the torment of grief and suffering, and medical procedures, maybe you shouldn't read this book. I lay my emotions bare to let you know that what you may be experiencing from losing a loved one is not much different than my heartache. All the upheaval that you're enduring through your loss is okay, anyway you choose to express it.

As a book on immediate grief, I write a lot of my emotions and moods through poetry, which you will find here. I've written poetry in the past but am mostly a book-length story writer. With Ron's passing, a new door has opened and my feelings pour out in verse. The poems aren't presented in any chronological order following occurrences and changes that I'm going through. They are written whenever emotions and feelings overwhelm me or when my mind dwells on something painful and expresses what I'm feeling through words. They are like *snapshots of turmoil welling up at unexpected moments.*

I hope I have written the kind of poetry that you can *feel*. All poems and essays are my own except where the author is noted. I've filled in some blanks of Ron's and my life together, only for continuity. What's important here is to assure you, the reader, that any grief you're experiencing, however devastating, is normal, and that you are not alone. I am going through it too.

Also included in this book are messages that I've shared from some friends of Ron's and mine, in their own words, who've also lost loved ones. My son, Dean Alan Deal (himself a magnificent writer), lost his father. You'll find some of his responses included. Ron's and my friends come from different countries and cultures. You may read varying opinions and outlooks about death, grief, and bereavement, and maybe varying religious practices. Some believe in an afterlife; others do not.

I have gleaned a lot of information for this book from listening to how friends have dealt with their grief processes and wish to pass their solutions along to others. My counselor, too, is a veritable fountain of knowledge and encouragement.

My hope is that you find something among these pages which helps you understand that your grief is completely normal, as you may come to understand from the widely varying experiences of a few others. Despite the anguish, we will all adjust according to what our life situations require for us to live with the memories of those we have loved and lost. Be open-minded and find the validation that you deserve.

PLEASE NOTE: It is my intention to donate a portion of the net proceeds from the first year of sales of this book to the **American Cancer Society – Renal Re-**

search. Get your friends to buy a copy. All this information can help anyone live through the bereavement period—whether for yourself, or to help family or friends.

Outside In

In the years before you
I felt like a loner
always on the outside looking in
I've never been a joiner
maybe that's why
but outside was a lonely place
Then we met
Suddenly I was a part of something
a part of you and me
no longer on the outside
but wrapped securely in your arms
building shelter from within
a place I'd never known
till you smiled sweetly
and wrapped your love around me.

1

BEGINNINGS

In the economic downturn of the late 1980s, I was self-employed as a business consultant, yet, due to the slow-down, my contracts were not being renewed. Companies were also laying off employees. I happened to be speaking to a friend, telling her that I had saved money for another trip to Kauai.

Sadly, I then needed to rely on my savings till finding other work. The friend suggested I meet an acquaintance of hers who also loved Kauai. I agreed; it would be like a breath of fresh air, being able to share with someone about that island paradise. Doing so would take my mind off my uncertain soon-to-be unemployed predicament.

Later, after speaking with him, she told me his name was Ron Holte and that he approved of her giving me his phone number. He lived in Sacramento. I lived in San Francisco, 100 miles away via a two-hour drive.

I waited a few days building up my nerve. On April 1, 1990, a Sunday, I called him, and we chatted with and about each other. Something clicked right then on the phone. It was a sense of pure friendship.

On Friday, April 6th, we met! I drove to his office in Sacramento. I was surprised how tall he was, 6'2" and about 210 pounds, with a little bit of stomach. He had a full head of the most beautiful, whitest hair I've ever seen. His warm brown eyes told me what kind of soul he had. That was what mattered. I learned he was 56. I was 49 at the time. After lunch, we walked around the Sacramento Capitol grounds, visiting the Vietnam War Memorial, where I located the inscribed names of two former high school friends.

Ron and I spoke on the phone every day. He called me. He was interested! We spoke about Kauai a lot. I did not wish to jump into this friendship too fast. He spoke about his work as a business Financial Consultant, managing accounting, taxes, and investments. I spoke about my self-employment predicament. He suggested I come again to Sacramento. He was sure if I would relocate, he could help me find work. On weekends, he performed accounting and payroll work for five different charities in the area. He knew people who knew people and had contacts through his regular work.

On April 21st, Saturday, I drove to Sacramento. He would spend the day showing me around and helping me get acquainted with the large metropolitan area. When he opened his front door, he held Mandy, his tiny Yorkshire Terrier, lovingly under his arm. Seeing him with Mandy lightened my heart. It was a fun day and our conversations always included Kauai. It was amazing how much we both knew about that island. I learned he would visit the island once or twice a year in spring and fall to play golf, get away from his extremely busy work life, and relax.

As the days and weeks passed, my work contracts

ended one by one. I continued to watch the newspapers and visit an employment agency for job openings in the Sacramento area. I drove up there for at least three interviews, traveling the two hours up and the two hours back in the same day. Ron didn't like that. My twelve-year-old 280Z had over 120K miles on it; he felt it wasn't as safe as I thought it to be.

We continued to see each other at least once a week. He didn't wish to put Mandy in a kennel so he could drive to San Francisco. He always put her into a kennel, however, when he flew to Kauai, and felt bad when she was returned to him one-to-two pounds lighter and weak. She was only ever four-to-five pounds. Due to his charity work, he couldn't get away on weekends.

Over time, we had become very close as friendships go. Ron provided a Shell gas card to pay for my trips. If my car should break down, he would pay all expenses. He paid to have my car checked for security. Early on, I stayed in a nice motel, at my expense. I insisted, but my savings were diminishing very quickly and, as if he knew, Ron offered to let me stay in his house. I could take the second bedroom.

We had grown fond of each other. I wasn't looking for a physical relationship and he respected that. In my heart, I knew Ron. I felt his soul and his need for understanding, and for someone to allow him to be the person he was, big heart, pensive, introverted and all. We grew tight like magnets drew, and proved that love was much more than sex.

One day, he stunned me with a question: would I like to go to Kauai with him in June. "I have a time-share," he said. "You can have the bedroom. I'll sleep on the sofa."

I was shocked, couldn't say much except, "I couldn't afford such a trip."

He simply continued. "You can have the car too. Just drop me at the golf course and you can go visit your friends. The only thing I'd like is for us to have dinner together, be in each other's company in the evenings."

He had a lot of Air Miles to use for himself and didn't mind paying for my fare. We flew to Kauai for one glorious week. We hiked the Kalalau Trail and saw much of the island together, taking each other to places either hadn't been to or known of. He slept on the couch the first night. I could tell he did not rest and, so, we slept together in the big king bed for the rest of the time.

A memory I have is that when we hiked the Kalalau Trail on Kauai's North Shore, he told me to slow down. I was rushing to see a view over the cliff to photograph. In the middle of a muddy, sloggy section of the trail, I slipped and almost went over the one-thousand-foot cliff. The only thing that saved me was that I grabbed at a tree root and hung on. Ron's expression, one that I've come to know so well, was a non-believing silly half-smile that reminded of his warning though he didn't say a word.

On July 4th, he again asked me to move in with him. I had not found work; my savings were nearly depleted. He kept reassuring me we would be fine in this relationship we'd begun. He said if I later wanted to return to San Francisco, he would set me up securely so I could safely resume my life in the Bay Area.

In the early morning of July 27th, Friday, I followed the moving van to Sacramento and a new life. Ron came home at noon, bringing lunch. By the time he returned home that evening, my few possessions were in place. Dishes, clothes, curios, assembled as if I had already lived there for some time. Even my business files were in the third bedroom, which he allowed me to set up as my office.

I began working for Ron immediately, helping him with the charities. When I saw the amount of work he did, it made my head spin. I took over managing his personal office while he traveled. One evening, I told him I would pass on a salary and make do with the household allowance he was providing. He was thankful, because he wouldn't have to lay off the cleaning lady (he didn't want me cleaning *our home* when I was doing so much working beside him).

We worked closely and drew closer and closer emotionally. Life went on like that for five years. In addition to working with him, I had time to fulfill my dream of a writing career—and was into writing my second book and receiving royalties.

His mother, with whom he was extremely close, passed away in 1992. Ron was truly weakened. At her gravesite, as they lowered her coffin into the ground and with Ron standing behind me, I felt a rush of emotion from him wash over me the likes I'd never felt before. Once her coffin was in place, he stepped away to a nearby tree. He couldn't bear to see them drop the lid onto her vault. It represented the finality of her amazing life. Of course, I went with him and found him shaking. I was glad to be at his side to see him through his profound grief. All I could do was support him emotionally while he dealt quietly, inwardly, with his loss.

During the next three years, we traveled, visiting

various Hawaiian islands. Getting completely away from our hectic work schedule provided him time to reflect on, and share with me, the loss of his mom. When Ron retired in 1995, we began to carry out plans to move to our island paradise of Kauai.

Wrinkles of Expression

We met during mid-life
You, mature and handsome
Me luckily retaining
some looks from youth
We aged gracefully together
as our faces matured
eyes wizened
reflecting souls
Now that you're gone
losing youth long forgotten
I miss your weathered face
rugged and durable
full of wrinkles of expression
eyes mirroring the soul
of one grown wise with age
It's your elderly features
I'll remember the most
because we grew old together
I can only hope
my wrinkled features
eyes reflecting my soul
show as much expression
of love and compassion
as yours.

2

BACK TO THE PRESENT

Ron suffered renal cancer in 2007, losing his right kidney, and again in 2008, losing his left adrenal gland. The doctor told him this type of cancer always returns after ten years—it will show up in the brain, lungs, bones, or all of them at once. I couldn't help wondering: it's good to be informed, but could the prognosis be programming him for future illness?

On November 14, 2020, after seeing his energy waning the past two years, and him complaining of an occasional headache, Ron collapsed. I took him to Emergency, where he was diagnosed with a brain tumor. Further tests revealed spots on his lungs and a tumor in his remaining adrenal gland. So started the four-month arduous fight to bring him back to health.

The radiation and immunology treatments were working! The first series of treatments had shrunk the tumors incredibly well. Continued treatments showed evidence that the tumors would be reduced to scar tissue and maintained so they would no longer grow.

Yet ... perhaps the treatments were too much for

his aged and weakening organs to endure. He would collapse while walking outside. One morning, he felt very weak, could barely hold himself up in a chair. For a third time, I rushed him to Emergency—and that was the start of the end of his life. Then, Ron's heart failed.

He received a pacemaker, which brought back his strength. His color was good, eyes bright, face full of hope. Yet, within one day of his circulation improving, the brain tumor filled with blood and hemorrhaged vast amounts into his brain, impairing all his autonomic responses. I watched him weaken and slip away over the next few days ... yet always hoped for a miracle.

On March 24, 2021, I fed him, massaged him, did all the bodily care necessities the nurses may have done if I weren't present. The last time I saw him before he went into coma, I knew he would not be coming home again. Still, I hoped, and remained in denial, all the while caring for him any way I could.

On the last day that he could actually respond, I got him to take several small spoonsful of chicken-noodle soup broth. He could barely swallow, but kept trying. I thought that offered a glimmer of hope, even though by then he'd lost the ability to speak. Before leaving his hospital room for the night, I spoke to him about the many fun times we'd shared, showed him a picture on my phone of the bougainvillea bush outside our patio, with its profusion of deep pink, magenta-red blossoms. He stretched his neck to see it. The man loved flowers ... and these would be the last flowers he'd see. I told him how much I loved him and sang to him the endearing long-ago song we'd made up secretly between us.

In the hour before I left, he became even more

still, sunken into his bed with eyes closed. I watched him failing. I asked, "Does Mary love her Ronnie?"

Surprisingly, he nodded by barely dropping his chin once.

Then I asked, "Does Ronnie love his Mary?"

Again, his chin dropped once.

It was hard to leave because I didn't know what I would find the next day. I wished I could have stayed with him overnight but the rigid COVID pandemic restrictions wouldn't allow it.

The morning of March 25th, his doctor found he had slipped into an irreversible coma. He was totally unresponsive, vitals barely registering. The doctor ordered an emergency, third CT scan of his brain. They found it flooded with blood from the hemorrhage.

The doctor told me that due to the condition of his brain, he had only a couple of days to live, three if we received a miracle. I immediately transferred him to Hospice of the Valley, Eckstein Center here in Scottsdale, where he could get the care and end-of-life treatment that he deserved.

Ron slipped away peacefully thirty-six hours later at 6:15 the morning of March 27, 2021.

Weathering Life

I lay in my warm bed
weeping and shivering
like a hypothermic
in a home that's warm
but now feels cold
lonely and empty
even though
all you are is still here
in everything I see and touch
waiting for your return
like any other day
But you will never be here again
to share the life we've built
Now you lay in another space
becoming colder and colder
in your warm bed at Hospice.

A Highly Evolved Soul

Your sometimes timid smile
your warm brown eyes
reflecting layers of feeling
show me the deepest reaches
of your heart
and mind
I want to remember
every expression you offered
especially the gentle caring
the understanding when I didn't
the patience of a man
with a highly evolved soul
who chose to share
the best years of his life
with me.

The only way to take grief out of death
is to take love out of the world.

— RUSSELL M. NELSON

3

FLEETING MOMENTS

After Ron passed, with myriad fleeting thoughts, came the realization that to get through the torrent of emotions, I had to figure out a way to survive. Life had changed and left me numb. I knew no way to proceed. All I could think about was that Ron was gone. The shock and immediate loneliness were unbearable. What might happen to me now? I had no answers.

My friends' attention to my condition and emotions was the only thing that kept me buoyant. They helped me get through one day to the next, then the next. Having been through their own grief processes, they were familiar with the shock and denial in which I was lost. My counselor's advice and assurances during the phone sessions was a lifeline.

Not until after I established the cremation process, after filing retirement papers and the required death certificates, did the denial begin to wear off. Then, amid the pain and numbness, sweet though now sad memories began creeping in.

From time to time, I'd have fleeting thoughts of special occasions when words were unnecessary. Ron and I read each other's thoughts, actions, and expressions better than being expressed in plain English; like that first expression I'd come to know from him when I fell on the Kalalau Trail on Kauai.

Another memory was when he attended a conference in Reno, Nevada and I'd accompanied him just for fun. We happened to be on the golf course when we smelled rain coming. I don't golf but drove the cart for him and managed to get in some photographing. We'd barely gotten started when the drizzle began. Then it rained harder. Before we knew it, we had sideways rain. The roof of the golf cart was no help. It was funny at the moment and we laughed heartily. We looked at each other. Without saying a word and at the same time, we both motioned with our heads to continue. Needless to say, we were soaked by the end of the 18th hole, avid golfer that he was.

Hilarious memories such as those made me sad, realizing the life we'd known could never be again. Even good memories brought tears. Many others were moments I wish could have been different or ended differently.

Nevertheless, nothing can be changed now ... and all are moments I will cherish forever.

Watching

Your facial expressions
particularly
during your illness
I will remember always
I would find you watching me
You'd smile so sweetly
gentle looks of love
appreciation
making my heart flutter
Every glance a different
communication
The way you tipped your head
or rolled your eyes
or looked away timidly
knowing you were caught again
If you were reading
when I entered the room
you'd close the book
to watch me
Slyly, I'd catch you
Were you worried
how I'd fare
when you were gone?
Your expression mournful
melancholy
a knowing sadness
behind those loving eyes
expressing your heart
now etched into my memory
of how you knew
how ill you were
wondering if the end was near
and in watching me

I could only guess
you were lovingly drinking in
as much of me as you could
not knowing
how much time you had left
to live.

31 Years

Ten days short
of our anniversary
you left me
Through 31 years
all successful
amazing days each
incredibly love-filled
even to the last
soul-searching end
that took you
Still, I cherish the end of it
equal with all the rest
The toil and strife
the bitter fight
against unrelenting illness
Those days exemplified
the courage
indominable will
you always had
with love conquering all
to the heart-wrenching
end.

When The Time Came

You nor I wanted to be kept alive on life
    support
I didn't know if I had the courage to end
    your life
When the time came

I watched you weaken, no longer functioning
quietly slipping into a coma
When the time came

The doctor said your condition was irre-
    versible
gave you two, three days at most to live
When the time came

It was now my decision to stop monitoring
    you
let you go peacefully since you weren't in pain
When the time came

I summoned my strength to follow your
    wishes
told the doctor to end all monitoring
When the time came

I carried out my promise because I love you
But found no satisfaction in pseudo-courage
When the time came.

4

WISE WORDS FROM MY COUNSELOR

After I wrote the poem, *The In Between*, I sent it with a message to my counselor. What follows was our email exchange. His message is powerful and applies to all who endure similar loss.

The In Between

Too quick
You were here
now you're gone
the in-between
a memory
experienced
in bits and pieces
that comprise the whole
of meaningful life
but finished
all too soon
a plan
not of our making
leaving behind

**a residual of
longing, loneliness
and heartache.**

Me: Sometimes I think I may never heal.
Counselor: Thanks for feeling comfortable enough to reach out to me. Maybe we ought to think of what you are experiencing as something other than an "illness" from which to "be healed."
You have entered "sacred pain" and are not suffering from an illness, rather from a bruised soul and a crushed spirit—you are one whose reality has been shattered.
The pieces of that reality are slowly falling back into place, perhaps fitting a little differently and forming a different image of the reality that you and Ron had before.
Mary, it is true you will carry the pain of Ron's loss for the rest of your life. But Mary, that pain will change over time. It will feel differently, not as acutely or as sharply. Do you remember the analogy I used of the rock in your sock and the same rock in your pocket? It's the same source of pain, but it feels differently in your pocket than it does in your shoe. After a period of time, the rock's presence in our pocket can become unnoticeable to our senses, unless we reach down and feel it, and are reminded of its presence—kind of like car keys or a billfold in your pocket—the pain you are feeling now will change.
You're bravely entering into your pain; you are asking questions of it, and are expressing your pain through verse. This is hard work, but I also know that it is cathartic for you. Please continue to do so ...

...but also take time out for yourself. Put the pen down and go for a walk, watch the hummingbirds lighting on the ocotillo, listen to the woodpeckers ... not asking you to divert, merely to incorporate other activities so that you are

not continuously and totally immersed in your pain.
Balance.

One day you will write poems whose endings will reflect a new but different reality—you will be reflecting upon other things Ron has left to you other
than the longing, loneliness, and heartache identified
in your well-written and expressive poem. You will
remember the memories, the times you had together
in Hawaii, and the long hugs that gave you both so
much security and warmth. You will not only remember but also realize that connection with and to
Ron that you could not dissolve or end if you tried. *He
has left you his heart.*
Remember e e cummings? The poet? *I Carry Your
Heart with Me* is one of my favorite poems. I think it
captures, Mary, what we are aiming for in realizing in
Worden's 4th Task: "finding an enduring connection
with our loved one while embarking on a new life."
I wish you Peace, Mary. I am sorry it hurts so badly,
but you are doing the work that will bring you
through your grief to a different place than where you
currently find yourself. I'll be here for you till we get
there.

<u>i carry your heart with me</u>

i carry your heart with me (I carry it in
my heart) I am never without it (anywhere
i go you go, my dear; and whatever is done
by only me is your doing, my darling)
i fear
no fate (for you are my fate, my sweet) i want
no world (for beautiful you are my world, my
    true)
and it's you are whatever a moon has always
    meant
and whatever a sun will always sing is you

here is the deepest secret nobody knows
(here is the root of the root and the bud of
    the bud
and the sky of the sky of a tree called life;
    which grows
higher than soul can hope or mind can hide)
and this is the wonder that's keeping the stars
    apart

i carry your heart (i carry it in my heart)

— E E CUMMINGS

Missing Parts

When things began to crumble
seeming bleak
you appeared in my life
like a gleaming spark
when fanned
erupting into a healthy flame
burning away problems
replacing them with
patience and wisdom
solutions I hungered for
but didn't know where to find
what I needed or even wanted

You became my mentor
offering solid solutions
and understanding
to questions and actions
that puzzled or evaded me
Now time has flown
successful years have passed
sadly, as have you
I haven't become you
though you have satisfied
the missing parts of me
allowing me to accept what I needed
rejecting what was not right for me
not allowing me losing sight of myself

Now that you're gone
the part of you that I have allowed
to strengthen me
will live on
my way of keeping you in my life

keeping you remembered
so that many are reminded
of the glorious soul
that inhabited your earthly shell
I hope you can see me
from the other side of the veil
feeling satisfied in how you completed
this part of your purpose here
knowing I am humbled and thankful
in how you made my life whole.

5

HOPE IN UNTRUTHS

Without realizing it, we all improvise ways of keeping hope alive. Hope can heal. Hope can bring about miracles. Sometimes.

I Lied To You

Knowing you
paying attention
to your quiet moods
no longer difficult to read
I could tell
when you worried
Would you make it
out of the darkness
the chasm of illness
back to normalcy?
I offered encouragement
"We'll get you through this."
You smiled weakly
sweetly in appreciation
"We'll get you strong again
go back to Kauai.

Play golf there
yet another time."
Your eyes
expressed gratitude
for encouragement
but also showed
exactly what you knew
that I lied to you
offering something
to dream about
to keep hope alive.

A New Revelation

A stunning revelation cast up by a memory
jolted my thinking, clarifying confusion
After your second CT scan
a nurse had said,
"He has bleeding in the brain."
She said nothing more
With proper care, I felt we could stop it
You were resilient, your brain would heal
your regular treatments were working
miraculously
But your words keep playing in my mind
bringing understanding, epiphanies
Again, I remember you saying,
"Let me die. Let me go."
With that memory came a new revelation
I realize the surprise I saw on your face
when I said, "I can't just let you go."
that we will help you heal
You knew no one had told me
what they told you after the scan
that with the bleeding in your brain
you were slowly dying.
You said, "Let me die."
because you thought I knew
that I should stop the caregiving
You realized I hadn't been told
To comfort me, neither did you tell me
and continued to allow me
to show my love as I needed to do
You needed my comfort more
needed to feel my love in your last moments
because you wanted to slip away
without having to see me cry.

6

PARTNERS ALWAYS

Note: Susan Yamamoto was one of Ron's golf partners on Kauai. She lost her husband in 1993. At the time of writing her thoughts on March 7, 1996, shown below, her Rick had been gone three years. This is how Susan dealt with her grief. At the time Susan wrote me after Ron died, Rick had been gone 28 years ... and she still misses him.

SUSAN YAMAMOTO: LOOKING BACK

I can look back and see how time has healed my aching heart a little bit, compared to when Rick first died. Actually, I was in shock for quite a while – like most people who lose a loved one – but that's good because it helps us get by.

I was not in the right frame of mind for quite a while. If I read something or had something read to me – like my detailed letter from my lawyer – nothing sank in. Reading it even a year later made me realize that I couldn't make major decisions since I couldn't comprehend things 100%. Only now can I say that I feel more in control of things.

After about twenty-seven months, at the time

that I left California for Hawaii, did I feel okay about putting Rick's things away from his side of the dresser. Up to that time, I had his toothbrush and the clothes that he'd worn the week that he'd died still hanging where he left them. I needed those things around, because it was as if he were still at home; it was very comforting.

Some people get rid of everything right away, some take longer, like me. Since each person grieves differently, it's okay to do whatever you feel the need to do. Don't let someone force you to do something that you don't want to do. One thing I suggest: wait a while to permanently get rid of your spouse's things. *Don't rush*.

Many times, I wanted to stay in bed and not see anyone or do anything, but once my parents passed, I had to continue living because I had two daughters to care for. It really helped me to go to a bereavement group, as they could understand what I was feeling. They also helped me figure out some of the feelings that I was confused about. For one thing, I got angry with Rick for leaving me to do everything by myself. It wasn't fair and I resented him. I did feel guilty about feeling this way but found out that it's quite common. Also, feeling down when special days approach, like the anniversary of their deaths, birthdays, wedding anniversaries, or other significant days, is quite common.

Whenever I felt like sharing things with Rick about the girls, I found that writing letters to him in a journal really helped. It was my way of talking to him. I also put together a book about him with words from friends and family, his resumes, and anything else that concerned him. This proved very healing. I wanted anything and everything with his name on it because I missed *hearing it*, writing it, and saying it. I discovered that lot of people don't even mention his name anymore; it's like he never existed and that really hurts me. He was so much a part of my life that it's difficult not thinking and talking about him.

Even now, I still miss him and there's a big emptiness in my heart. I really miss the kind of relationship one has with a spouse. I do have my children (thank heavens for them) but it isn't the same kind of relationship that I had with Rick. Besides being my husband, he was my very best friend. Now, I feel that I have lost both.

No one knows how I truly feel except those who have lost their spouses. My parents and sister and her family really don't understand – I take that back – I think my dad knows how my girls feel, as he lost his mom when he was thirteen years old, but he doesn't know the loss of a *spouse*.

I talk to Rick and even ask for his help and guidance ... and many times I get the help I want. I have even felt him touching me after he died. I was with a friend (Rick's Hospice volunteer) who was doing Reiki on my back. I felt a touch where she hadn't made physical contact. She verified it wasn't her but said she was going to tell me that Rick was sitting there beside me.

I dreaded the first anniversary of his death. I planned to celebrate it with the Hospice nurses and volunteers, our close friends, and my parents. There was a nice luncheon at my home with everyone sharing special memories of Rick. Before that, at the six-month anniversary of his death, I had brought a donation to the two places that really helped him and I have brought donations to the Hospice that helped him on the anniversary of his death. It's a good way to give back for all they did.

I talk with my daughters about the possibility of marrying again. We've been able to joke about it but still talk seriously. While I cherish my independence, I do miss being with someone special to talk to and share my life with.

Realize that grieving takes a long while. Remember: tears are healing and the harder we grieve, the faster we heal.

WITHOUT END

Missing you comes from so deep inside of me
I cannot fathom an end to this heartache.

7

BEYOND MY CONTROL

The following poem is a *metaphor* describing the horror that ripped through our lives and tore Ron away the moment we knew the end was near. I have never felt such helplessness, panic, and sheer devastation in my entire life, and I could do nothing to keep the inevitable from happening.

On Tentative Ground

The ground shakes on the mountain
Loose soil and mud begin to shift
like a slow flowing river
Rumbling roars across the valley
Earth trembles, rocks bounce in all directions
Monstrous boulders break loose
unimaginable forces crashing downhill
claiming all in the unstoppable slide
I look for you across the valley
caught on tentative ground
"Stay!" you call to me
"Stay on solid ground!"
just as the shifting earth beneath your feet
claims you, sweeps you away
in a torrent of surely unimaginable sorrow
I watch the forces rip away the ledge
beneath the precipice where you stood
Without you, the earth has changed its face
Numbed but hearing your last words
echo above the din
on solid ground I'll stay
in this place we found together
until some benevolent force
claims me in my own torrent
and brings us back together again.

Hidden Gems of Wisdom

My guilt of placing you
in Hospice
was eating at my
emotional stability
I tried everything possible
to extend your life
now, in the quiet empty moments
after the desperate jumble
instruction and conversation
doctors and nurses
and trying to understand you
when you began to lose
your ability to speak
I suddenly remember
hearing you struggle to say
in a quiet but garbled whisper
"Let me die. Let me go."
I didn't hear you then
didn't want to
even thought you were testing
my loyalty and endurance
How selfish of me!

Now riddled with guilt
after placing you in Hospice
I realize you knew the end was near
still I put you through more tests
trying to get you to eat
and exercise your limbs
selfishly trying to save your life
for me
but you had already faced it
were ready to go

Now you must finally be at peace
resting in Hospice
as your words float back to me
like hidden gems of wisdom
letting me know
I had finally done the right thing
letting you go

8

AT THAT VERY MOMENT

Disappointment and guilt plagued me after Ron's passing. I should have been with him. I could have been holding him, giving every last bit of comfort possible. Though time has healed some of this disappointment in myself, I will always remember that I could have held him when he chose to leave. It had always been my intention.

NOTE: A cathartic experience happened in a follow-up to this poem and can be found in the chapters titled *Motivations* and *A Major Epiphany*.

A Wounded Bird

I watched you
near lifeless, unmoving
barely breathing
My heart wrenched
as I fluttered around your bed
like a wounded bird
not wanting to dump
my jumble of emotions
onto you
I wanted to hug you
hold you
but I didn't
for fear
of interrupting your peace
It is one of my
biggest failings
I should have held you
picked up your shoulders
held your body close to mine
You may have felt me too
one last time
Not doing so
one of the biggest mistakes
of a wounded bird.

I sent the poem, *A Wounded Bird*, to my son, who also writes heartfelt poems. I explained about my starting to write everything in verse. This was his response ...

DEAN ALAN DEAL

"I love when you write! It provides a sense of openness and continuity to our rushing and tumultuous thoughts.

"Emotions in our head are kind of like numbers: most of us can only hold four-six numbers in memory and trying to do an equation in our minds is problematic.

"Emotions are like that. We can't sort them, can't see them all, and can't put them all in order within our minds only. Our intellectual and emotional *buffers* are relatively small. But paper and pen allow us to record, order, examine and, most of all, apply an understanding not found in the tortured miasma of thought and pain and regret that storms in our heads."

When I recounted the moments of my experience, as described in the next poem, *That Wee Small Voice*, some friends told of their experiences. Each said the same thing: the dying person chooses when they want to leave.

In relating some of these experiences, I'll use some fictitious names, though the experiences are true.

Barbara lay beside her husband, holding him to assure him she would be near when he needed her, though he seemed alert and ready to rest. She watched him go to sleep, attentive to his steady breathing for nearly half an hour. She had barely drifted to sleep when something woke her. When she checked her husband, he had died, as if he had waited for her to go to sleep first.

Janie's husband, Frank, had a major stroke. He was admitted to the hospital. Frank told her to go home and shower and have breakfast before returning; he would be fine. She left. In the car, ten minutes later, she received a call on her cell phone. Her husband's heart had stopped and he simply slipped away.

(My family experience.) I was in Maryland on my way to England when I was notified that my father had died. Dad's lungs had collapsed, totally unexpected. He had always seemed strong and healthy. It was Christmas Day. In good spirits and forever positive, Dad had told my brother to go home and celebrate Christmas before returning to the hospital the next day. My brother went back to stay with him that evening and Dad seemed peaceful, his vitals stable. Returning home after midnight, my brother learned Dad had passed away at 1:00 a.m., shortly after he had left him.

As I prepare this manuscript, something I have not yet mentioned was that while I was a home-caregiver for Ron with brain cancer, so too was my brother, Charley, a caregiver for his wife, Dottie, also suffering from brain cancer. August 16, 2021, my sister-in-law passed away. My brother related the experience . . .

Charley had sat at her bedside for days, knowing she was slipping away. He wouldn't leave her, always checking her vitals and assuring she was comfortable. However, my brother's property was situated in the Caldor fire that raged through an area of California for a time. His hilltop community was nearly encircled by raging flames. He was worried that they wanted everyone to evacuate; how could he leave with his dying wife and all her monitors?

He remembered that he'd left his phone on the kitchen counter and needed it beside him at all times, waiting for an evacuation order. After checking Dottie's vitals and seeing no change, Charley went to the kitchen to retrieve the phone. While there, he wanted to feed his four cats and Doberman that were prancing and yowling to be fed. However, he experienced the strangest feeling and knew he had to return to Dottie. Back at her bedside, he realized her breathing and heart monitors were no longer showing signals. He bent down and found her no longer breathing; she had passed away once he'd left the room.

(An added note is that, strangely, in addition to both my brother and I caring for spouses with brain cancer, Ron passed away a few days short of our 31st anniversary. Likewise, Dottie passed away a few days before their 31st anniversary.)

The experiences I've heard all point to what

people repeatedly say: the dying choose when to leave. I'd heard many more stories like the ones I've related. Some say those dying don't want us to be present and feeling sad. That may be why Ron didn't tell me himself that he was dying.

With the exception of a few instances, from all that I've been told, most people wished to be present during their loved one's crossover ... and weren't.

That Wee Small Voice

Two nights after I put you in Hospice
I woke in the wee small hours of morning
from a troubled dream
remembering something I'd forgotten
In your struggle to live, days earlier
you faced that you were losing the battle
You had said, "Let me die. Let me go."
I had thrown that to the back of my mind
never wanting you to leave me
unable to face reality, that you'd be gone
From the dream I heard you say those words
I kept repeating them as I woke
to finally realize you had been ready
long before I could let go
Now you were telling me again it was time
At that moment
I wanted to lay beside you in Hospice
hold you close and give you comfort
Instead, I went to my computer
pouring out my sadness in poetry
dedicated to you
yet always wishing to be with you
I stopped writing, dressed hurriedly
then suddenly received the phone call
I never wanted to hear
Had I heeded that wee small voice within
When I first heard it
I would have rushed to you immediately
upon awakening
been there when you crossed over

My guilt consumes me
I could have held you one last time

And you would have known
I was always there for you
Later, after much anguish
With the brilliance of one of your
pieces of advice, I realized
you had told me in my dream
you knew you were leaving
that no matter what happened
Whether or not I was there
Just let you die, let you go
Without sadness or guilt
In your way through the dream
You came to say goodbye
We had been together at your passing.

9

WHEN THE REAL HEARTACHE BEGAN

My heartache began long before Ron passed away. From the onset of this new cancer, as I watched him weakening, I had to hide my emotions and remain positive to help him keep up his spirits and hope. I began to know the meaning of numbness. I remembered his former doctor's prognosis years ago about the cancer returning and feared the worst.

The following poem came to me when I was at the lowest ebb of emotion, when I couldn't think clearly, drowning in my sorrows. Reading this again and again over time helped me to see how low I'd sunk and that I needed to help myself if I was to help him at all. Regardless of all the good advice and guidance available, I was the only one who could help me and, ultimately, him.

With the passage of time, long arduous months, I've come to understand much more of my grief process by revisiting the following poem. After helping Ron through his transition, and being able to unhide my emotions, I began (more recently) seeing the truth I'd dredged up as I wrote this tragic verse.

Now I am no longer that emotionally low and, finally, on my way to a new sense of normalcy, whatever that may be.

Fire Without Flame

Stars fall like ashes
Sunlight stiff and cold
The universe howls
but there is no wind
Only descent
into an abyss
with no escape
into a fire without flame
in the prison of my mind.

A Lifetime of Training

Life's lessons prepared you
with a body that never quite
worked right
that taunted you
gave cause for concern
Yet you lived a successful
long and busy life
overcoming the shortcomings
of physical imperfections
But in death
one last lesson
the pain, the heartache
of shutting down
your soul preparing to leave
a lesson you handled graciously
from a lifetime of training
never complaining
sweetly smiling your goodbyes
positive to the end.

10

PLAYFUL NAMES

Ronnie came to be known as *The Black Swan* in his circle of friends. He read the book, *The Black Swan: The Impact of the Highly Improbable*, by Nassim Nicholas Taleb, and completely agreed with its tenets. Here's one review comment about the book:

"A fascinating and challenging critique ... I thoroughly enjoyed this remarkable author's outside-the-box mix of thought experiments, stories, and epistemology."

— EDWARD O. THORP, AUTHOR OF
BEAT THE DEALER

As much as Ron talked about this book, and him becoming known as *The Black Swan*, I can truly say I have not read it. Now, in hindsight, I will. As much as a black swan is present in our lives, it's my belief that Ron used the symbology to send me a message from the other side. I wrote about it here.

The Black Swan

I rise just after midnight
four days after you left
on April Fool's Day
a day you refused to play jokes
not that your jokes were ever brutal
Through jumbled thoughts I beg,
Why can't I get a grip after losing you?
Drawn to my computer for diversion
to stem the flow of tears
and ever-saddening thoughts
to join the world for a while
through watching videos
finding treasures under water
rehoming pit bulls
pictures of birds you posted
anything benevolent to bolster my faith
that life can still be rewarding
The first video that flicks into view
two healthy black swans
teaching their tiny gray-feathered Cygnets
to jump into the water to learn to swim

Like a message from you
who represented your business self
after the book *The Black Swan*
your Facebook logo a black swan
a photo I took, by the way
I watch two beautiful adult swans
encourage their babies into the water
They'd float, it was safe
One last Cygnet refused
surely fearful of taking a chance
The parent continues to encourage

until the last tiny newborn
jumps in, joining the family again
floating effortlessly together
Seeing black swans at my dark hour
was that your answer to my plight
unspoken message from your world beyond
encouraging me to jump right in
and start a new life again?

11

THE HAUNTINGS

From the day he left this earthly plain, I have felt Ron near. I would feel a nudge, see something move when it shouldn't, hear his voice, smell his tangy *BOD: Really Ripped Abs* cologne, hear noises related to him, and other inexplicable experiences. I would detect the smell of his natural skin oil. It was as if something were blowing a breath up my nostrils. We all have a certain body odor, yet, the actual smell of our clean skin is different. When I hugged him and placed my face against his neck, that unique smell of his skin was what I breathed. I'd detected his fresh scent numerous times in the first couple of weeks after he left.

The rational part of me says this could be my mind playing games with me. Am I creating these experiences to help sooth my torment? Does my mind protect me this way, leading me to believe Ron is still with me, and thereby easing my increasingly dismal outlook? Do traumas such as these take our minds beyond the brink of reality, as we perceive it?

Sounds of You

Walking down the hallway
and through our rooms
I remember the sound
of you pushing your walker along
At times other household noises
sounding eerily similar
send chills down my arms
making me wonder
if you're still here
and will I see you
in one room or another
But you are gone forever
from this home we shared
Still I'm wondering if it's you
playfully haunting my days
and teasing my memories.

Voices Like Glue

Some of us much aggrieved
hear messages
voices, phrases
from the great beyond
Our dearly departed ones
speak to us
like echoes repeating
out of the void
But what if it is
some unknown corner
of our minds
conjuring
a latent aspect
of the healing process
to help us through
the broken-heart syndrome
and fragmented life
voices like glue
reconnecting
everything shattered
Is it only our minds
in protective ways
speaking to us
in words and phrases
our loved ones used
because while living
they had become
so much a part of us?

12

A LONG-TIME FRIEND

Sherry and I met years ago in 1997, in an online writing group and have remained great friends since, though we've never met in person. When I had open heart surgery, she kept updates posted on my Facebook page. Through that time, she came to know Ron and they got along famously. She and I have always promoted each other's work. Another forever friend.

SHERRY RENTSCHLER: ON GRIEF

When I was a teen, I used to wonder where the expression *good grief* originated. How could grief be *good*? Wasn't the sorrow, the anguish, or the loneliness considered terrible? Were we supposed to feel good about feeling sad?

Then at 17, I tasted my first personal sorrow – the loss of my best friend in a car accident. Terry Lynn was my summer friend, someone I saw on vacation and who became my life ally. The daughter of my mother's friend, she was the mirror of my youth. When she died, I felt the sudden, jerking emptiness of her loss, immediately missing her laugh and our shared joys. I caught my first glimpse of grief's purpose, but I was too young, too bruised to comprehend it.

Her loss taught me to appreciate the experiences we shared and relish in the memories that kept her real and alive in my mind and heart. Though 50 years have passed, and I can't remember the sound of her laugh or the feel of her fingers laced with mine as we ran down a sidewalk, I still feel the joy of her when I eat custard ice cream or hear certain pieces of music she loved. The loss of a close friend brands the strongest, unique joy to our hearts and allows us to keep the love ever fresh. That's why grief can be considered *good* – for what it gives us in our tears.

The Flip Side

(for Terry Lynn who died too soon in 1971)

Every year at summer's crest, I mourn
the loss of life and bond made of immortal
  youth,
pink cotton curtains, lemon rinse, and
life lived at 45 rpm.
Bare-armed and cross-legged,
two sets of baby-doll pajamas told
horror stories punctuated with
popcorn and nervous giggles. We searched
for our individuality, stumbling through
black lights, glass beads and Ouija boards.
Dream by dream we made a future
of proms, poetry and friendship.

Summers by the Potomac River, nestled
in the Appalachian foothills, promised
custard cream, wild strawberries and
stolen green apples. Our hope was
eager, simple and honest. But death
came early, random, and anonymous.
They buried our friendship ring with you,
leaving me alone to live out our dreams –
Girl Scouts and dates, college and marriage.
It was lonely without you; no one could quite
remember how good custard tasted in the
  heat,
how sweet giggles sounded in the dark,

Or how bright blue eyes sparkled at 45 rpm.

(Flip side refers to a vinyl record's *B* side, or rarely used side)

SHERRY RENTSCHLER: LAST LESSONS

My father died from lung cancer. He opted to stay at home with my mother instead of going to a hospital. He was on morphine and gradually faded away. The last night he stirred enough to have a last moment of semi-awareness before he moved on.

My father was my hero, and watching this terrible cancer debilitate and then steal his life cut me harder than anything I'd ever felt. The man had survived the Great Depression, flying in the Korean War, losing multiple jobs, moving several times across the country. He'd raised two daughters born in different generations and worked in NASA's Apollo and Space Shuttle programs. Dying in the dead of night from such a dire illness seemed distinctly cruel ... and anonymous ... for such a dynamic life.

I confess, I started grieving for him a year before he died. From the day he told me he had cancer and wasn't going to get treatment, a part of my life stopped. I suppose the purpose of my grieving was to remind me of the lessons that he'd taught me even with his death. I spent my life trying to make him proud of me, and in the end, he gave me the best lesson of all: to understand death.

It enriches me to this day and, with his hand on my shoulder as I move through life, I am better for my grief. His last lesson to me was the most profound and the one I think I needed most for the rest of my life.

Last Lessons

I miss my father.
Even now I marvel at his faith
blazing through cigarette ash,
cancerous sighs and a morphine stare.
Dying,
he lingered with shining will,
with the glimmer of renewing dawns
like steel in moonlit, if weaker, nights.
He was no less beautiful to me
than a dove's cooing or my mother's
gentleness, tending his hope
(and hers)
like the roses blooming from their life
(and children).

"Remember,"
his jaw commanded against the pain,
"There's no shame in clay feet,
or stumbling and falling, weary.
Determination made the Pyramids
indomitable
with hard work, mud and -
yes - ashes.
Strength is made from heart's mortar,
in character, not hormones."

I miss my father's calloused hands in mine,
lessons at age five and forty-five.
His last and best found when he was lost.
Love isn't only what we have while we're
    alive.
It's the strength we're given to stay behind,
and say goodbye.

NOTE: Both poems published in *PAPER BONES* by Sherry Rentschler © 2013, at Authorhouse

The love you take
   is equal to the love you make

              — THE BEATLES

The love you give
is equal to the life you live

— MARY DEAL

13

MEMENTOS FOREVER

As I sorted through Ron's belongings to dispense as he'd instructed, I came across a little old box of items that looked to be something one might find in an auction storage unit. When I looked inside, it brought tears to my eyes. This was a box of mementos that meant the most to him. He hadn't yet unpacked some of the items after our move here nearly four years ago, some of which he'd usually kept on his desk. Him neglecting to do that told me how long his memory had been slipping. I sat on the edge of the bed, holding these ancient treasures in my hands, trying to feel his presence as I wept silently.

Treasured Mementos

Your tiny box of treasures
aspects of personality
Your mother's baby picture
a great woman remembered
Your one baby shoe
the other your mother kept
A blue high-school pennant
that always waved boldly
A toy Southern Pacific train
your first job while in college
A preserved dollar bill
a step into a new life
A cache of money clips
a joke about ego
A tiny clay golfing bear
your first hole-in-one
A Viking ship pendant
a symbol of strength
treasured mementos
to which I now add
my treasured mementos of you
a life preserved in pictures
your thumbprint on a gold pendant
a lock of your hair
an urn of your ashes.

Never More

My heart is broken
My soul weeps
filling the void
you left
with tears
and longing
never more
to hold you
heart to heart
One broken heart
left never more
feeling whole.

14

A REASON FOR CRYING

Weeks after Ron passed away, I went to bed still crying myself to sleep. Following my wise counselor's coaching, I asked the pain why I was crying. Probably needing to escape, I promptly fell asleep, lost in the jumble of thoughts as I prayed for guidance.

In the morning, I woke without tears. The reason I cry came to me upon awakening; I cry because I'm *SCARED*.

I came to rely on Ron for everything. Not that I gave up my own thoughts and decision-making. We discussed most everything major. We found solutions, or compromised when we needed to. We came to rely on each other for input; one or the other had information that made our decisions right.

I'm scared because all these years I'd relied on Ron for balance. From age 17 to 49, I relied on myself, made mistakes, swallowed pride, and continued on. It was a struggle but also rewarding, raising a son, sacrificing so I could be a successful single mom and he go on to be successful too. It worked. I've supported myself through it all, not having the type of mind to get caught in ruts in the road. Till now.

When I met Ron and saw how we influenced each other in positive ways, I came to rely on him, if only for assurance I was doing right things. I came to rely on sharing everything with him so that we were both part of anything major. We both expanded every aspect of our lives. He became my mainstay, reassurance that I no longer had to struggle. My independence remained intact, now shared with Ron, who admittedly needed me to give him purpose.

When Ron passed away, all that security was stripped from me. I must get back to the independent person I used to be, which now seems like a different person, totally foreign, and I'm scared. Long before Ron left, we knew we had some big decisions to make.

We began being bombarded with community assessments, the likes only a wealthy person could absorb. Every homeowner in this community association becomes an open bank account from which the association may draw. We knew this was a possibility when we moved here. Now, it seemed too much a burden.

Originally, we thought this would be the last home we would know. We had settled in. However, if we had to sell the home to protect our retirement savings, then we would. We talked about finding another cozy place, not necessarily locally. We talked about returning to Hawaii, even planned a one-month trip back to Kauai during September 2020 to see if this was doable. Then the COVID pandemic hit and stopped most travel. We changed our reservations to June 2021 ... but November 2020 was the first time Ron collapsed. Whether we'd make the June trip became questionable.

Now, along with all-consuming grief, I need to

sell our home and get out from under the mountain of looming debt. Had Ron lived, we would be making plans to sell. One thing is certain: I will not go back to Hawaii to live. Every memory of Hawaii I have since living in those beautiful islands with Ron, includes him. I do not wish to go back to make new memories without him. I have no idea where I will relocate.

When I asked the pain why I cry, I received an answer. I cry for Ron no longer living. I've lost my partner, half of "us". I cry because we can't live as long as we want, to prepare for an end as we wish it. I cry for loss of Ron's wonderful and surprising solutions to problems, because now I must make major decisions *alone*.

I feel weakened, thrown into a new life I wasn't expecting so soon.

I'm strong and have managed on my own for many years. Yet, having known the strength of the security Ron provided, and now having it suddenly stripped away, I'm scared. Life, overall, is different, but this is no longer a time for tears. Ron strove to provide me a good life once he was gone; I will protect all that we have lovingly built together.

From now on, I must make these decisions myself. As much as I wish to stay in this home representing the life we built together, I must begin the process of leaving. I must find another place to move and buy a home. I can only hope I'm making correct decisions. That is why I'm scared. In the emptiness of this physical world, I hurt and cry for the stability I had with my wonderful Ron.

Everlasting

Life is temporary
Love is eternal

Half the Cycle

To be born
means to die
a rationale
simple and clean
What is it
that binds two people
becoming one
that when one dies
the other grieves
forgets
the rationale
the cycle
of life and death
What invisible force
causes one to feel
one half is gone
What binds two people
to become one
then only half again
when half completes
the cycle?

15

AN UNDERSTANDING NEIGHBOR

Rita Vacca is a pillar of our small cluster community. Her life experiences have made her resilient. She was with me from Day One and helped to keep me thinking correctly when grief would wash over me in uncontrollable waves.

RITA VACCA: HER PERSONAL EXPERIENCE WITH GRIEF

When I first learned the news about my husband's condition, I went into denial. My thoughts became jumbled.

- What is going to happen?
- How long will this go on?
- Why is this happening?

Then, I moved on to acceptance and I looked for and prayed for a miracle. I learned about insidiousness and realized attitude is everything. I changed to fight mode and learned to stay in the moment. I cried in private because of the frustration and fear of it all. At times, I felt I functioned on automatic pilot. Time did not mean anything any longer. Dealing with my husband's illness was all-consuming. Then, as time progressed, I realized the end was near and what all that would mean.

Alone, I screamed a primal scream. It came from my total being. When the end came, I was numb and functioning instinctively, more so than ever before.

I am weary and totally exhausted.
I am not sure if I am functioning totally.
I feel like I am losing my mind.
I push on because I do not know what else
    to do.
I make mistakes.
I'm not to be trusted to make big decisions.
Nothing seems the same.
But I can't figure out a new way to be.
I cry a lot.
Sometimes I stop and can't go on.
This all passes.
Over time I adapt to the loss.
I feel different and slowly heal.

I found watching movies about grief helped me feel I am not alone in this. As time goes on, I realize I am doing okay and feel the energy of my husband around me. I now cherish the memories and feel very thankful to have had this person in my life for as long as I had.

I am no longer afraid that I will forget him ... and know I will *always* remember the life we had together.

Kept Alive

The face that I adore
the heart that is so pure
those hands of gentle touch
the feet that carried you
that body of strong endurance
will never again grace this earth
but kept alive
in all my memories
that play again and again
in a mind and heart
that will never forget you
So, if loving you through grief
makes me hurt
then I choose to live
the rest of my life
in pain.

16

STOP RECYCLING
THE PAIN

Often times, we grieve for both the physical and emotional anguish our loved one suffered. We need to write out our thoughts and feelings. Yes, it's okay to talk about what our departed ones endured, but by writing, we get it out of our system and into a format that we can *see*.

What I've found is that by mentally recycling what Ron endured, especially in his last days, is what brings on my crying bouts. I feel guilt that he had to endure great emotional suffering about his life ending when mine would not. In a sense, we survivors punish ourselves for not feeling our loved ones' pain and struggles with them. In thinking and rethinking their suffering, we're trying to alleviate our guilt at not being able to help them, but instead only exacerbating our guilt and pain.

We will still feel pain and cry more. The times I cried hardest was when I realized what Ron must have thought about knowing death was imminent. Ron was quiet, never an unnecessary word. When he spoke, it was worthy. When he faced imminent death, he went with the flow, never complained, never offered a sign or expression of frustration. Always that sweet half-smile encouraging look that said, "We've got this." It was that special expression that told me not to worry, that we had planned to face together whatever happens to us.

Remembering those subtle reminders still tear at my heart. He must surely have kept negative emotions tucked inside.

We ultimately realize that we can sink into our sorrows and guilt, or we can choose to stop reliving the suffering that has finally ended for them and realize that it needs to end for us too. That is always what our loved ones want for us. We live on with their love and memories inside our hearts.

Finally, we get a grip on our thoughts and emotions. Our *self-talk* has changed to more positive attitudes. We confront what we need to do to start over. The change could go unnoticed, till one day we realize we're feeling more at peace and truly moving forward. We stop punishing ourselves by trying to relive their pain. We decide to do what they wanted us to do: to move ahead and be happy.

In my case, joy and relief come partially through writing my sorrows. I can still hear my counselor's words:

"I encourage everyone to write out their feelings, their thoughts. You're a writer, Mary. You should be writing your process. Write letters to Ron. Keep a journal, if that's something that appeals to you, but write."

With the release I've had, stepping away from writing fiction to writing about my personal life, I sincerely encourage others to record their thoughts and feelings, no matter what they may be. Most likely ...

... you are the only person who will ever read those writings.

Say what you need to say. Express your true feelings. Writing can renew your strength. Yet don't be afraid if you back-slide into negativity and regret. Stoically determine to get yourself out of it again.

What I realized from writing is that my thoughts shifted over time from my sorrows to telling Ron about what I had planned for my days and how much his memory affected how I now live. Writing gave me a chance to sort my activities from day to day. It showed measures of my progress toward getting my life back together and was encouraging.

When I wrote the following poem, I realized my thoughts had changed; they were directed away from self-centeredness and became more focused on what Ron had endured. It also reminded me that I had to stop thinking about how he suffered because that's what made me sad. Writing this poem taught me to look beyond my dejection and to move on.

Grief Far Greater

I sit quietly enduring the pain of grief
What happens to me now?
I'm numb; what do I do, where do I go?
An enlightening thought comes to me
Grief is selfish with thoughts all about me
Reality slams into my consciousness
makes my heart quiver with truth

What about you
when lapsing into a coma?
Surely you still have thoughts
The days prior when you couldn't talk
your hand gestures spoke clearly
a mind still functioning

What about you knowing you're slipping
    away?
Do you feel panic or quietly accept the in-
    evitable?
After a successful lifetime ending in peace
    and love
knowing you are helpless to abate the on-
    slaught
the scourge that overpowered positive
    treatments,
are you scared even though you are
    speechless,
resigned to go quietly not showing your
    suffering?

How do you deal with leaving loved ones?
Your hand squeezes, fingers touching my face
tell of your abiding love

from halfway on your journey to the great
      Hereafter.
Do you miss me already? Are you sad to leave?
Did you hear me when I told you
you'd find no more illness, only pure love and
      peace?

Can you feel my love pouring over you
the only comfort I can give?
Do you cry silently as I cry now?
Do you know I will weep?
Do you worry about what will happen to me?
Do you wish to stay, not wanting the end so
      near?

You suffer quietly unable to speak
your hand entwined with mine
neither wanting to let go,
your mind filled with longing to continue
      with life
but accepting that you're the one who'll be
      leaving
Surely, in silence, your grief is far greater than
      mine.

What Do I Do

What do I do with the love
that I have for you
now that you're gone?
My emotions feel stunted
even though I send love to you
in my thoughts and prayers.
What do I do with this love
that has no end?
Will the Angels carry it
up to you?

17

SAGE ADVICE

When you have supportive family or close friends who offer sage advice, write down what they say if it's spoken to you, or read the words sent to you; read them over and over, and let them help you find moments of peace.

Eighteen days after Ron's passing, I still slept fitfully and woke up crying. When I wrote my son, Dean, this was his loving response:

"I tell people who work for me when they are having a life crisis:

'Your most challenging and painful life event will end up being a repository of hard-won experiences and your first point of reference for the next mountain you must scale and conquer.'

"You know better than I, Mama, that all the experience you have won in your life is dearly bought. The vantage point from which you view life now is the best place you have from which to find your next path out of the morass of pain you are in.

"When you begin your journey on the new path, the one you are on now will give you greater reference, greater impact, but without the ravaging pain of a new wound.

"You will be okay; you will thrive and this current challenge will add to the wealth of your wisdom and help you tackle the rest of your life.

"I love you. I am here."

Peace

Nothing else matters
but to love your partner
your family
and let that love
spread to others
with whom you share
your life
If we all do that
touch others' lives
humanity could know peace.

18

FINDING ANSWERS

Christina and Tony lived across the driveway in the little cluster of homes in our community. We became fast friends. After Ron passed away, they made themselves available to help me in any way they could. They assured me that my counselor would help me understand everything. Tony also took me to my two COVID appointments. They didn't want me driving alone, should I have a reaction. They both knew what I was facing in the days ahead.

Here is Christina's own experience with grief...

CHRISTINA HANSON-PIERZCHALSKI: THINKING THROUGH THE PROCESS

No matter how sudden or expected death is, I struggle with grief as many others do. Initially, I feel selfishly sorry for myself. What am I going to do without this person? How will I be able to go on? After time, I ask myself how can I have these selfish thoughts? Is it right of me to think this way when the person is suffering? I would never want anyone in agony to remain here on this earth, just so I wouldn't feel the loss of them not being here with me.

How have I mentally and physically dealt with the passing of my loved ones? I have sulked. I've spent days in bed, under the covers, ignoring the outside world and phone calls and texts from loved ones checking on me. When I finally had the physical capacity to return to civilization, I would purposefully avoiding sound cheerful when speaking. I'd smile less, etc. If I did those things, people might think I'm not grieving, that I don't miss who I lost. But how long do I remain this way?

Over time, I realized I couldn't live like this forever. My loved one would not want me to live like this, to mourn their nonexistence. They would want me to remember the great times and all the wonderful memories we'd made. Friends, family, and therapy helped me embrace this realization and new thought process. Talking helped—it helped immensely. I didn't feel like I was the only one who experienced this after a death. Others felt this way, too, and they have survived and are thriving. That's when I knew I could too.

I purposely choose every day to celebrate their life. Whether it's in prayer, following a recipe that they used to, or just talking out loud about them. I surround myself with pictures of them and that makes me smile. It's a conscious effort I make. I never want to forget their memory.

I keep them alive in my heart and my mind *every* day.

Undone

Your demeanor changed
When many might feel
panic
you became calm
a little withdrawn
Your subtle facial expressions
told of deep introspection
I knew then
you were reviewing
the highlights
of a life well lived
knew you were
bravely positioning
as the end drew near
perhaps processing
what might be left
undone
Your final expression
as you passed over
told that resolution and peace
were yours.

OPENING OLD WOUNDS

If the friends who support you the most seem to shy away once in a while, it may be because they have been experiencing their own grief and *your* grief may be opening old wounds. It may simply be that they feel for you and cannot stand to see you cry.

Mentally repeating memories of a loved one dying can easily throw us into a downward spin. Yet, somehow, we hope that the more we think about it, the less hurtful it might become. At times, we find ourselves on an emotional roller coaster, unable to control thoughts. It's then that we must decide whether to remain in the pain or understand it and move on.

When I was visited by some friends, we talked about our spouses' deaths. I found a few visitors would talk only about losing their spouse, drawing all attention back to their own memories. I knew they needed to talk. My situation gave them a chance to pick up the pieces of their own grief, and to be able to put them to rest.

Grief knows no limitations. Anything can spark a visitation from our personal trials, no matter how much time may have passed. We survivors must be patient with our dear friends, who mean well. We must give them a voice, just as they allow ours.

Something that helped me greatly was hearing how my lady friends moved through their own misery. I found validation for myself through their experiences. While we all grieve differently, we also all have love locked in our hearts for our departed loved ones. Through my friends, I've learned that love never diminishes. As my counselor said, *"... the pain takes on a different quality, but we still hold that same love in our hearts."*

Ever More

Remembering all our years
not a spat, no real differences
just compromise
respecting each other
and always love
sweet gentle love
filled with hugs, kind words
and heartwarming surprises
once shared in peace
ongoing happiness
till fate separated us
leaving only memories
to sustain the future
only memories now
to keep our love alive
till we meet again
never to part ever more.

20

MOTIVATIONS

(**W**hat follows was mentioned in the earlier chapter titled, *At That Very Moment*.)

Standing at Ron's bedside a few hours before he died, I desperately wanted to pick him up and hold him. Something kept me from lifting him to me. I started to bend forward a couple of times, then stopped. Once, I placed my hand behind his neck, almost lifting him, then stopped when I felt his cervical vertebra jut sharply. He always had extreme neck problems and they were exacerbated the thinner he got. I thought, in his weakened condition, I might hurt his neck, or worse, break it. He had become exceedingly thin and frail. Like I wrote in the poem, *A Wounded Bird*, I now feel guilty for not having held him close. He might have felt me holding him one last time. It could have been a last comfort to him.

My only consolation is that, as I leaned over him and spoke softly to him, I gently rubbed his face and pushed his hair back. I stroked his arms and lightly rubbed his chest. I touched his skin wherever I could, hoping he felt it all, hoping my love poured through my fingertips and my voice as I spoke and sang softly to him.

Days after he was gone, I had to have some closure for this strange notion that I couldn't pick him up. My counselor had a suggestion as to why I could not bring myself to hold Ron's body and reminded me about the Bible, when Mary Magdalen wanted to hug Jesus. He said to her, *"Touch me not for I have not yet ascended to my Father."*

When I entered Ron's Hospice room the morning he died, I could feel his presence hanging in the air above the foot of the bed. I was aware of many other beings around him. Angels?

"Oh, Ronnie!" was all I could say as I looked up into the space. Then, I sat on the side of his bed and held his hand and talked to him. Although deceased, I rubbed his chest, his arms. I even looked at his feet and touched them. I always gave him pedicures when he was too weak to do it himself. This would be the last time I'd see him. I wanted to see as much as I could, one last time.

I still remembered that I had decided not to pick him up. I did manage to place my upper body and face close to his and take numerous pictures. Repeatedly, I kissed his face, his lips, his closed eyes. I took pictures, but it was as if I couldn't take enough. Some didn't turn out, yet I will never part with any of them. I have a photo editing program that removes blurring and other issues from pictures. It is my plan to make every single picture-perfect as possible and keep them forever.

As I placed my face close to his expressionless mask, I was fully aware that he was watching me from above. I yearned to hear his voice, for him to tell me he was okay, even though I believed that he was free of his ailing body and finally healed. I stayed in the room for quite a while and felt him always present with other Spirits.

Ron had a patch on his left arm and still had the cannula, the IV base stuck into his right arm. I wanted to do something, anything for him, one last time. I left the room and found the nurse, and asked her if I could remove the patch and cannula.

She said, "We can't let you do that. We're responsible for removing everything before he leaves us."

"Oh, please," I urged. "I want to do something, any last thing I can do for him. *Please*."

The nurse left, then came back right away. "We can let you remove the bandage but you cannot touch the cannula because of the needles. We cannot allow it."

I understood and rushed back into Ron's room. He was still floated above the bed. I moved to the other side of his bed. I'd long been aware how paper-thin his skin had become. He had developed edema, fluid trapped in his left arm. The fluid had simply broken through his thin skin and leaked out; hence the bandage. I took time to gently ease the tape away from his skin.

All the while, I knew Ron was watching, understanding, appreciating, and loving me. I felt his presence. I don't exaggerate this. I have felt the presence of other family members over the years. It's a matter of being open to the possibilities and wanting them to transpire.

The nurse had told me that Neptune Society would be around in one and one-half hours to collect him. I stayed the better part of an hour, then left to give the nurses time to remove the cannula and to prepare him for pick-up. Were they also responsible for removing the pacemaker? I sickened at the thought of them cutting open his half-healed incision to remove it.

Leaving him was the hardest thing I have done in my life. It would be the last time I'd see or touch him. I paused by the door of his room and went back several times to kiss him goodbye. Then, with waves of futility washing over me, I looked into the air space above the foot of the bed, clasped my hands, and said, "Goodbye, my Ronnie. I will love you forever."

I then fled the place that would send him away from me. I couldn't stay, couldn't bear seeing them slipping him into a body bag and zipping it over him.

I don't know how I drove home, but the next thing I remembered was needing to get out of the house. I walked outside in the yard in the bright morning sunlight, sauntered aimlessly in the mutual driveway of our cluster of homes, crying. When I went back inside, I remember sitting and staring at the pictures on my iPhone of Ron in full coma at the hospital and the ones I had just taken at Hospice. By the time I roused, night had fallen. Still, I sat, weeping in the darkness.

The Hugs

We had a peculiar habit
strange to others
emotionally sustaining to us
Didn't matter where we were
in front of the fireplace
beside my easel
on the patio watching birds
in the kitchen
tasting your delicious soup
happened anywhere
for any reason
sometimes for none
but just to hold each other
We loved to hug
We'd cling together in silence
holding sharing love
wrapped together never moving
till one of us had to let go
or lose our balance
Now as I close my eyes
wrap my arms around myself
I can feel our hugs
as if you're still here
Of this I'm certain
I'll remember the feeling
this love I'll never forget.

21

EMBEDDED IMAGES

One of the most difficult aspects of moving through grief is waiting for the images of trauma to recede into the background of memories. I remember the look on Ron's face the third and last time I rushed him to Emergency. As we waited to be seen, I realized he had gone into great distress, was not responding. I screamed for a nurse. She determined his heart had stopped and called a Code. Suddenly, seemingly out of nowhere, other medical staff filled the room.

With Ron in his wheelchair, they raced to a private treatment room. Six people picked him up by arms and legs and each side of his body and tossed him onto the gurney. They had to move fast. The look on Ron's face in his semi-conscious state: surprise, fright, confusion, looking but not seeing. Yet, I am sure he understood what was happening. His facial expressions are embedded images that haunt me.

He came around a bit as they swiftly cut the clothing off his body. We took such great care of each other through our lives. I could only stand by helplessly and watch him endure the shock of it all. It took an hour to get him stabilized. Needles and probes and wires and IVs and oxygen! The expressions I saw on his face were uncertainty of the unknown. I still remember his face going through changes as if all this were happening in real time today. I can only imagine what it felt like for him; it traumatizes me to know what he endured both physically and emotionally.

After stabilizing him, they left him lying nearly two hours until they found a hospital room for him. The facility was full to capacity due to the COVID urgencies. Ron was weak but speaking, though not much. He simply lay still. I could see his mind working; he knew how grave this latest episode was.

Depths of Despair

In the depths of my despair
I wonder what it's worth
A lifetime of struggle
rewards or disappointments
from beginning to end
a full life experienced
perhaps leaving a legacy
hoping our lives leave the world
a better place
In the end we leave it all behind
as we are forced to let go of caring
and to look forward
hopefully without trepidation
to a new life beyond this earthly realm.

22

DEATH OF A FRIEND

A few weeks after Ron passed away, I called Linda Watson, asking her to let her husband know that Ron had died. Her husband, Forest, and Ron always talked investments while we lived on Kauai. We weren't in touch much after they moved back to the Mainland, except that Linda remained on Ron's Facebook page.

To my surprise, Linda had her own sad news that was another shock to my traumatized nervous system. Now, Linda and I console each other as much as possible through the Internet. The following are some of the conversations Linda and I shared, published with permission.

LINDA WATSON: EXCERPTS FROM CONVERSATIONS

Linda - Mary, that is sad news. I have terrible news as well. My incredible Forie passed away Jan 26. Too long and painful to write, and I'm still too devastated to be without him after 45 years. I feel as though I've lost an arm and a leg. Moving slowly through this period of grief. Take good care of yourself, and I will pray for Ron tonight.

I have great faith, and Forie became a Christian in his last years; I found some comfort there, for sure. But I'm very lonely and that will take forever to get over. Beg God to let you have a sign from Ron that he is okay. I begged much before Forie died and have had some incredible experiences where I know it was him. You will feel it, and treasure it when it comes. Bless you and bless Ron. Be kind to yourself and go slow. The emptiness is like nothing we've ever known.

Oh yes, yesterday and today were awful cry days. This process is not a straight line, but a forever line of ups and downs, distinguished by the amplitude that comes from time. I still cry almost every day. Be patient.

Mary – I am shocked to hear this. Am so sorry. Ron and I were together 31 years. I credit my counselor for helping me not lose my mind. I can image the grief you are enduring. Please take care of yourself and, likewise, I will pray for Forest. Thank you for letting me know.

I am patient. I have those days too. I just finalized the Obituary for the Garden Island newspaper. Then, I broke into unstoppable tears. I think I'm doing fine, then I feel guilty. Then I tell myself, "Just stop!" The waves then wash over me again. I'm a very strong person. You are too. But strength and being tough have nothing to do with it. I lay in my bed at night talking to Ron about anything that comes to mind, till I finally sleep fitfully. My nights are filled with dreams, some horrible, but some give answers. Yes, I am being patient and, at the same time, watching a process I can't control.

Linda - Perfectly and beautifully said, Mary. I am your sister during this journey; it's a tough road to travel, but ladies who have gone before us assure me that it gets easier. I want to believe them.

Mary - (Linda invited me to come to her home in California.) What a gracious offer. Thank you for that. I probably can't make a trip. I'm expecting Ron's Death Certificate by the end of the week. Then, I will take care of his taxes and other business. He had his hands in more things than I knew. Now, it's up to me to put an end to them. We really thought he would beat this illness. He was improving rapidly. Now, I must also dispose of his many belongings according to his wishes.

Linda - You're newly in your grief. Don't be afraid to take a day here and a day there just to be; even take a day to be in your jammies and do nothing. I took over a month before I saw my kids because I was so flat. I had Forie's funeral five weeks after he died because I knew I wouldn't be able to do it sooner. Best decision I made. When we were all together, it wasn't a cryfest, but a calm, sweet, remembering time.

Be easy on yourself. The grief you feel is the reflection of the Yang (Yin/Yang) of the joy and love you felt for him. Take a break, breathe, write your thoughts, give yourself permission to be where you are. It's going to be a long, long journey for us, Mary, but we can do it. We *must* do it. That's what Ron and Forie would want us to do. Live elegantly and well; squeeze more joy out of life as they wish they could do more of. We must carry on for them because we love them.

Mary – (I sent Linda a copy of my poem, *A Wounded Bird*, presented earlier in this book. This was her response.)

Linda - Without disturbing him too much, I did crawl slowly into bed with Forie in his last hours. I was holding his head in my arms when my parish priest called and prayed over Forie and begged me to let him do Forie's service at my church. We don't do everything right at the end because we are paralyzed with grief and fear. I have a few huge regrets but dwelling on those is no good. I believe that Forie knows that I wasn't capable of doing better at those moments, but that I was doing the best I could.

Having regrets is normal, but not profitable. It fixes nothing. But they linger and I know that to be true. Be kind to yourself. Ron would want that for you. What you have left is to live in a manner that will make him proud. Breathe, pray, relax. God will take care of everything if we trust in Him.

After the nurses cleaned him up (Forie), after taking all the tubes and IVs and everything off him, I had them dress him in a nice golf outfit. I laid in bed with him for an hour or more, just whispering my thoughts and feelings and memories. We are grieving girls right now, but we are lucky girls to have had our beautiful men.

We didn't invent widowhood, Mary. Millions of

women have walked before us, in destitute situations. We are still lucky. You are normal to swing between feeing okay and feeling like a wet rag. Don't beat yourself up over it. THIS IS HARD TO GET THROUGH. No joke! Be as kind to yourself as you would be to someone else in your position.

I have Forie on the coffee table in our bedroom, by his place on the sofa, where he would sit, one doggie on each side of him.

When he was in the hospital, he said to me when I was sitting on his bed, holding hands and talking, "You know what I would like, Linda? I wanna go home, sit in my spot on the sofa, cuddle my doggies, have a fire and have you sit beside me, and we have a nice glass of wine together." I'll never forget it as long as I live.

This is all very hard to live with, all the questions, all the doubts, all the regrets, all the mistakes you think you made, all the unanswered thoughts. I pray that time softens these *barbs* that puncture our souls many times a day. We are powerless now to change the past. We have to believe that Ron and Forie's love for us was so big that they now know all the truth and are at peace with everything. **Grief is not for the dead; it is for the living.** Forie and Ron coming to us in their heavenly ways now shows us their compassion and understanding. Whatever we think our sins are, our boys have forgiven them, just as God does. They are trying their hardest to just send us love every day. We need to be open and recognize it and live in it.

Mary - I can't sleep. I've lost eleven pounds in the month Ron's been gone. Am using my wakefulness now to tell you of a vision from Ron. First, you need to know the last flower Ron saw was a deep magenta-red Bougainvillea just outside our patio. (He loved flowers and birds.) When I showed him the picture on my phone of the profuse blossoms, as weak as he was, he craned his face forward to get a better look. His eyes opened wide. Something else you need to know before I explain. I am debating to get a pendant with his thumb print permanently embossed on it. Am debating whether to be frugal at this present time and get the small one, or splurge and get the larger one.

Three mornings ago, I had a dream that continued even as it woke me. Someone out of sight on my right side threw deep magenta-red Bougainvillea flower petals toward me. They came from high on the right and cascaded down toward and in front of me. In the back, among the smaller petals, were small oval-shaped gold disks that kept moving past. In the center of this presentation was one large golden oval disk, just hanging there, gleaming brightly in the sunlight. It simply hung there while the smaller ones passed by.

Linda, you tell me. The magenta-red petals represented Ron. The small gold disks passing by represented the small-sized pendants. The large single gleaming disk hanging there in the sunlight in the center, was Ron's message to get the large one!

I will eventually be painting that dream image on canvas. I now vow to paint every image he gives me. This is amazing.

Linda -Monday was three months for me – a HORRIBLE day. I cried at everything. I'm just starting to come around after a huge down day, climbing out to see the sun again.

LINDA WATSON: MY THOUGHTS – MY GRIEF

At 10:24 am, Tuesday January 26, 2021, the light went out of my world.

Over a month earlier, I prayed Forie would make it to Christmas and the New Year. The night before January 25, the doctor came to talk with me, to tell me that my love wasn't going to make it through this.

Me: What do you mean? It's a ruptured appendix. I know his lungs are bad (he was on the lung transplant list @ USC) but … Doctor, you don't know this man. He's just a very sick man with a very scared wife to you, but you DONT KNOW HIM and that he's the strongest man in his constitution that you've ever met. He's a genius, a dreamer, an adventurer; he can conquer anything, if you give him a chance. He's built big buildings, raised four children, built boats and sailed across many oceans, cooked beautiful dinners, designed our wedding rings as well as many gorgeous homes. He's a state senior golf champion and he's a father, grandfather, and great-grandfather. He's been my EVERYTHING for 45 years! You CAN'T give up on him.

The doctor was silent with tears welling in his eyes, just looking at me. He noticed the cross hanging around my neck. "Where do you go to church, Linda?"

I told him, "Sacred Heart."

He nodded. "Me too." And then, silence.

I had worked for Hospice for 10 years. I had been

there for my mom's last days, and I knew what this meant.

Me: "So, now it's morphine?"

Doctor: "It's the kindest way."

Me: "Oh no, this can't be happening."

SILENCE.

Doctor reaches toward me and hugs me.

SILENCE.

Me: (a nod and a hand squeeze)

The first bag of morphine, Forie could hear me and respond by squeezing my hand. Johnny Mathis songs, sailing songs, Elvis gospel songs. Prayers and remembering how he finally decided that Jesus was the real thing. My grandma's rosary over his chest. Me talking all night about all the incredible moments of our life together and how we were in our last voyage together, through the dark night, and that he would make landfall alone this time—to the most glorious of all landfalls.

I put on lipstick and kissed the outside of his snow-white body bag that lay against his cheek. I wanted everyone to know that this man they were touching was SO LOVED.

I don't know exactly how I drove home. I think Jesus was driving. I went to bed –

for days . . .

He came to me: a heart in my coffee foam, his arms holding me in bed, his voicemails on the phone. He made me stay alive. My children made me stay alive. The planning for his funeral made me stay alive. Our doggies made me stay alive. I started to see that there was still love around, that there was something to stay alive for.

Now, I'm six and a half months into this. There is the strangest mixture of anguish and joy, like oil and vinegar. They don't mix well, but together they are a recipe to dress up a salad, like dressing up a broken heart. My body and soul hunger and ache for him. I ache to hold him, make love with him, cook dinner for him, hold his hand while we walk, to rub his neck at night. My soul aches to hear *I love you*, to be happy to drive home from the mall, to hear his laugh and hear him call my name, see him cuddle the doggies. A deep, deeper, deepest ache . . .

> I live to make him proud.
> To make my children proud
> To make my God proud.

That's all I know for sure. I stand at the threshold of the door between grief and gratitude. I haven't stepped thru the door, but I am still STANDING there.

Every journey is different, except they all contain love and a broken heart.

I wish you Godspeed.
Linda

Well-Loved

If your heart is broken
with the loss of your loved one
then you were well-loved

23

FORGIVE OTHERS

Too soon, people will ask questions that seem cold and unfeeling, like, "When's the reading of the will?" Some see your grief and say, "Oh, you'll get over it. We all do." Or, "You need to move on now." The cruelest words I've already heard were, "Well, he was old. He was going to die of something sooner or later." These words cut deep and hurt.

Forgive these people. Some, who have never known grief, have no idea how deeply loss hurts and how confusing this experience can be. They may lack tact and the finesse it takes to deal with a person living through bereavement. They may never have known loss firsthand nor anyone suffering from it. Forgive them and avoid them if they persist. Try never to reply. Anything you say will come from pain that you already feel and could be just as inciteful.

Likewise, some of your closest friends may choose to stay away. The reasons vary. They don't want to see you hurting. Nor do they want to be put back in touch with any grief they may have suppressed in the past. As stated, many simply don't know how to deal with a person who is grieving. If these close friends have not contacted you after a length of time, when you are much stronger, contact them. They will know by your speech and attitude that you are getting on with your life. It is your right to grieve. Don't throw away friendships because you need to work through your emotions. True friends will be waiting when you contact them again.

Alternately, should someone choose to be happy that the person in their life is gone and they are glad to see them go, most likely that survivor is egocentric or holds a lot of animosity toward the departed. They have unresolved issues. Eventually, these people will need to seek counseling to understand their feelings, or their negative thoughts will fester like sores. For whatever reason, those who feel only happiness to be free of the departed are harboring a load of negativity. They feel no grief, but when these thoughts and emotions aren't dealt with, they have a way of coming full circle, like karma.

Moving On

Written into perpetuity
The errors, the failings
insecurities
right judgements
life sustaining heartfelt love
Nothing can be changed
Lamenting the past shared
with a departed loved one
keeps us stuck in grief
delays future happiness
blocking
a new reality that seeps in
pushing heartache aside
never forgotten but to become
a minute portion
of the larger scheme of life
and death
with past goodnesses
remembered brighter than all the rest
Moving on because we still live
in the memory of all things that were
of all things yet to be
taking their places in our lives
till our cycle like that of our beloved
completes.

24

DID I HEAR YOU?

Hospice of the Valley, where Ron lived his last hours, operates *White Dove Thrift Shoppe*. I had gone to browse and purchased a few beautiful picture frames for some of Ron's photos. As I was leaving with my purchases, a wee small voice in the back of my mind said something. I immediately repeated it mentally, but louder. I stepped outside. On the sidewalk, I shook my head, then repeated the words again. I knew that voice did not originate from my thoughts. To say the least, I stood in awe.

The words of the first sentence were sung, like old-fashioned music both sung and spoken. The second two lines were spoken words. Imagine singing the first line of this verse, then speaking the rest:

For the rest of our days: Live a good life
till we meet again

A little past three months after Ron's demise, I was sweeping and hosing down the front patio to take pictures for the sale of the property. I was wondering what he might think about me selling our wonderful home. Would he dislike it? Would he think me selfish and unforgiving? While I was visualizing him sweeping and cleaning our patios, I heard a voice in my head say:

Wherever you go, I will go too.

It was stunning to my senses. I stood still for a moment, replaying those words and that voice in my mind. It was the same distant voice that sang and spoke the first phrase that I had heard weeks earlier.

25
A FRIEND'S THOUGHTS

S am Woollard, Sr., and wife Hilary are a couple Ron and I met on Glass Beach on Kauai in Hawaii. Our friendship clicked immediately. They are from Yelverton, Devon, England. They make many trips to Kauai, where their family members come together from various parts of the world.

Sam and Hilary invited Ron and me to join their family festivities every year. We maintain great friendships to this day. Since they knew Ron, I asked if they would like to contribute some words related to how they may have dealt with loss in the past. What follows is Sam's poem of how he acknowledges his personal strength and dealt with grief through his belief system.

Indestructible
by Sam Woollard

I fear not death
For I can talk with ghosts
In my front room

They come as friends
To comfort and advise
And guide me back
on the path I chose
When I met them all before

We were not in body then
But on a higher plane
Together in Spirit
Deciding our next lives

We work together as a team
Each helping the other progress
Toward Nirvana
or what by any other name
We call God

Some of them are doctors
And bodyless they help to heal
By guiding others
In the laying on of hands

Yet other ghosts will tell of
Halls of learning
Where we can try to distill
The mysteries of life
Out of the universe

And yet they cannot take away
My free will to live
my present life
In any way I choose

My fellow ghosts remind me

In case I should forget
That life is forever
Never starting never ending

An infinity, a circle
That always was and always will be
Like me, Indestructible.

26

GETTING BEYOND
THE REGRETS

Those of us who grieve may come face-to-face with thoughts about how we treated those loved ones who have passed. Were we a negative force in their life, if only occasionally? Actions of the past may come up to haunt us. We will realize when we could have reacted more positively in various situations. None of us is perfect and, being human, are at times given to retaliation for what we may feel an injustice done to us.

Some may have reacted in extremely negative ways. Yet, after our loved one has passed and we harbor memories, we now feel sorry for some of our former reactions. We dwell on the negativity. Without understanding why these situations carry great emotion, anyone could fall into self-loathing. We pray to God and to our dearly departed for forgiveness . . . pray the torment in remembering the negativity will be washed away. We realize the harm of even the simplest unspoken negative thoughts.

. . .

What must happen in order to get beyond dwelling on regrets is for the grieving person to first forgive themselves.

All relationships, especially long-term ones, have many ups and downs. Grief has a way of forcing us to see errors made in the relationship. When we realize those errors and determine never to react in similar negative ways, we actually go on to live with more positive reactions and solutions; this is one of the greatest means of self-forgiveness.

In changing our erroneous negative reactions to situations, we have forgiven ourselves for past transgressions. However, if we fail to understand or admit our past errors and continue making the same mistakes, we have not forgiven ourselves. How can we forgive ourselves and move on if we do not acknowledge our mistakes and negative reactions?

When you're in the sorrowful throes of remembering how you may have hurt your loved one, admit you could have made better decisions. Admit you could have thought through your emotional surge before reacting in hurtful ways. Determine that you will never again be a person reacting in that manner. Not admitting this will keep you wallowing in sorrow and regret; admitting it enables you to move on and live a much stronger and healthier emotional life.

My Own Example of Forgiveness

Ron passed away at 6:15 am. However, I awoke before that at 3:00 am, after hearing him in a dream distinctly say something that he'd whispered to me days earlier in the hospital. His voice continued even as I woke.

I was so filled with emotion that I went to my computer and spent several hours noting my sorrowful emotions and all that I might endure surrounding his impending demise. By the time I began getting dressed to go and stay with him at Hospice, it was a few minutes after 6:00 am. I was half dressed when the phone rang at 6:20 am. I immediately knew what that meant and started trembling.

"Oh no! Oh no, not yet!" I declared out loud.

Soon as I answered, the nurse from Hospice confirmed that Ron had passed away at 6:15 am. I nearly collapsed, but hurriedly finished dressing. All the way to Hospice, I realized I should have gone to him the moment I heard his voice in and out of the dream. It was Ron telling me he was leaving. Instead of thinking about *my* emotions and *my* sorrow and going to my computer to write about it, I should have listened to my inner voice telling me to go to him. He was calling me and I didn't recognize that I should immediately rush to him.

I have no greater regret than this.

Yet now I wake up many mornings at 3:00 a.m. After weeks of doing this, I have decided to turn the 3:00 hour into something positive. I get out of bed and write essays, poetry, and passages for this book.

I failed to go to comfort my Ron at the 3:00 hour; that can never be changed. So, now I will turn these early morning hours into the type of writing from which others can read and benefit, and move through their bereavement—hopefully, with more wisdom and less suffering.

This has been a lesson in getting outside of myself, and the rush of emotions about me, and to think of others. Ironically, the one thing that kept me from going to him in his last hours – writing – is what I will use now to help diminish my regret, by helping others.

Real Love

Love doesn't happen in a lifetime
It stems from previous eons
eternities past
always was, is, and will be
It ignites
when twin souls find each other
in an earthly existence
Love endures
till one, then both have gone
from this lifetime
True love
real love cannot die
from temporary separation
Real love is what comprises
the soul of each
It is the heavenly spirit
like two lights merging
Then when one passes before the other
from their earthly odyssey
not until the one left also passes
does the eternal light of their love
join together again
as it should be
eternally in the Great Beyond
into and out of
earthly existence
re-joining together as one
throughout all of time
Always was, is, and will be.

27
WHAT IS
WALLOWING?

When the agony of sorrow consumes us, we need to acknowledge that intense state of mind and *welcome* it . . . and determine to get through it. Some of the ways we do that is by writing our thoughts, talking to our deceased loved one, or asking ourselves what the pain is trying to tell us. A reason for the distress exists. My very wise counselor told me if I ask the pain to tell me the reason, then purpose and thoughts come with clarity. We are then doing something to help ourselves not only to grieve as we need to do, but helping ourselves get through it. Grief will not end if we do not face it.

It's okay to cry. You should. You must. In the days and weeks after Ron died, I cried constantly. Many nights I fell asleep crying; mornings I woke crying. My eyes seemed perpetually red and swollen. During the days, everything of his that I touched prompted memories that hurt because they could be no more. Even living in the home we shared made me weep. His essence is still here, all around.

Regardless that we may cry constantly, we will need to move on with our lives. We must do the usual day-to-day tasks that are the fabric of our lives. Yes, we will do them through tears, so have plenty of tissue boxes sitting around.

Part of my day-to-day responsibilities is distributing Ron's clothes and personal effects to people he wanted to have them. In addition to saddening tasks like that, we both knew before he passed away that we couldn't stay in this place. Now, I want to stay here because this was where he last lived. I also know that once on my own, I must be frugal with my income till all accounts are settled. Unfortunately, that meant preparing this house for sale.

Fresh tears seem to come in waves. I set about taking care of daily tasks and keeping preoccupied. Then, something causes a painful memory and I sink into a multitude of emotions again.

As I go about selling furniture and other possessions, I cry a lot. I was deciding which of our many pots and pans I should keep or give away. I found Ron's big spaghetti pot that I gave him one year for Christmas. When I saw that big boiler, it reminded me of his love of pasta and ability to cook. Hugging that vessel like I would hug him, I slid down the kitchen cabinets to the floor, and wept. Needless to say, I will never part with that big pot.

Still, I see the essence of Ron going out the door with other belongings. I realize all that's left are precious memories and a few mementos. I also have faith that no matter where I am, if Ron wants to find me, he will be right at my side.

Carrying on with life, regardless of tears when emotions besiege us, is how we move through our grief instead of delaying facing those overwhelming moments. We may cry. We may weep. As long as we continue with the necessities of life, we are not wallowing in our sorrows; we are working through our grief. If we refuse to address the sadness head-on, regardless of the anguish, and we cease to function in your daily lives, then we are probably wallowing in our sorrows.

I've heard a couple sad stories about people who numb their grief with alcohol or drugs, or partying and putting on a happy face. Or they simply refuse to talk out their emotions and remain in a non-speaking, passive state. If you sit on the couch all day watching TV and drinking, numbing yourself, and never really know what's on the screen, you are wallowing in your sorrows. You cannot numb yourself forever, though some may try.

Once you stop denying yourself, the emotional pain will still be present, and you will need to work through it, however delayed the process may be. Grief never goes away. It's best to face it head-on to help it subside to a livable level.

One Last Time

I stand beside your deathbed
looking upon your empty shell
lying peacefully in last repose
your face relaxed in simple grace
I'll never see those calm brown eyes again
or feel your arms around me
I hold your hands
touch your arms
stroke your cheeks
kiss your lips
one last time

I walk through our home
See the bed where you'll never sleep again
The table where we enjoyed our meals
Your bathroom with all the scents of you
the closet of a man who knew how to dress
the office that still holds your busy vibe
a bookshelf of a voracious reader
a recliner with the blanket for your legs

Everything is as you left it
It's all I have for comfort
I remember every last detail
I know of you and sense you near
It feels like you'll come home soon
Your essence hangs in the air I breathe
Are you still with me but in spirit?
Will you come to me one more time?

28

IN YOUR OWN TIME

Fran Loando and I met years ago on an airplane, when we sat side by side. I was going home to Honolulu; she, who lived in Arizona, was visiting family in Honolulu. We quickly became friends and closer still after Ron and I moved to Arizona not far from her. Recently, when I told her about losing Ron, she contacted me daily and helped me occasionally get out of the house. I learned that Fran had lost her husband years ago. Here, then, is a recap of how she dealt with her loss and life afterward.

FRAN LOANDO: IN HER WORDS

I have never really had a full-blown sobbing, crying, breakdown since my husband passed away. I think sometimes I attribute that to the fact that I went to work every day, tending both to him in his illness and to our everyday life. Then came a time I had to put him in a home. After work, each day, I would be with him till it was time to leave for the night. I spent all my time with him, staying by his side, more during the last days of his life.

I went right back to work two days after he passed. I didn't take any personal time to grieve. I was exhausted physically and emotionally. I felt I had done all my grieving and had already came to terms with it all. Yet, some days for no apparent reason, I would get such a heavy physical feeling, powerful, overwhelming, as if someone were literally squeezing my chest. I could not breathe. I could be driving down the road on my way to work, or in the middle of a grocery store, at a gathering with friends, at any given place, it didn't matter. I would find myself in situations where I felt like crying really hard, falling to the floor, and yet I could not let myself let go. *I would not let myself go.*

Inside myself, I could feel the physical hurt of my mental and emotional pain! Like I was exploding inside my body! I kept telling myself that falling apart was not an option while living alone with very few friends. All my family was far away. I did not feel that I could let myself fall apart for fear that I would not be able to put myself back together again . . . for fear that I would have to have someone help me . . . for fear I would be dependent on someone.

Very few people in my personal life helped me through that awful, anguishing time of Greg's illness and death.

Some friends, and some of his family, removed themselves from us at a time in our lives when we could have used support. Over the years, I have come to conclude that some of those people are afraid of illness and death, and just rather preferred to remove themselves from any of that. Or just plain really never were our friends. Nevertheless, I didn't want any of them to know anything I was feeling. I wanted

nothing from them. Then, my thoughts became jumbled and confusing.

> So, now what?
> My life as I knew it was not ever to be the
>   same.
> How will I survive?
> Reality hit very hard.
> What to do?
> Where do I go!
> How do I cope and feel?
> Who am I?
> When will I ever feel normal again?
> I am not that person I was before.
> How do I cope, how do I create a whole new
>   life plan?

After a period of time of trying to figure out what
to do about myself, other than work, I began going
out to dinner, movies, bars. I traveled, mostly alone
but sometimes with a small group of people I had
met. Over time, I began enjoying this life I was
starting to create for myself. I became very comfortable being on my own. Yet, I found it difficult to com-
municate or form close relationships with other
people. Much later, I realized it was because none had
walked my journey. Unless you are with a person who
has had similar experiences, no one can fully understand your walk.

I began dating but none of those friendships
worked out. Likely, I feel I sabotaged myself, and
those relationships. I liked the company, but really
did not – or was not – ready to let anyone into my
personal life and space. My most precious friend was
my little dog, Makena. She really saved me in many

ways, was my best friend, companion, and reason to stay grounded.

I went to grief counseling, which was helpful in that I learned most of my emotions were a normal part of the grieving process. My *not shedding tears*, as well, was okay. I was doing my artwork, staying busy, involved with family, friends, and community! I was assured that being busy was one of many ways to let go of emotions, and to heal.

Many, many years later . . .

Years passed. Then, I met a man who I can honestly say was *different* and, in many ways, took me by surprise. Many, many years of friendship and conversations later, he told me he was in love with me. This caught me totally off guard, but it wasn't hard for me to realize I had the same feelings for him. We have become each other's support and foundation. We have fun, laugh, and enjoy making memories and adventures together. We continue to maintain a friendship, through a whole new group of friends I found easy to be close with; we all just kind of came together.

It is very true that time heals.
You never forget your loved one.
They are imbedded in your heart and
    memories.
Healing and peace will come to you. Just takes
    time.

In your own time

The Void

When laughter ceases
no speech heard
all movements stilled
eyes closed
breathing shallow
till it stops
What is left
but a void
the end of all things
life sustaining
meaningful
stripped away
A feeling of loss
with no recourse
never to be redone
Hopelessly waiting
for the universe
to fill the void again
with life familiar
cherished
but impossible
forever gone.

29
THE MOMENT OF DEATH

My mind often wanders in places many others wouldn't dare to go. I discovered a strange twist, perhaps only in my thinking to help me cope. I include it here.

As stated, in most cases I have heard the ailing person passes away when their loved one(s) leave the room. Does the dying person know when they are alone? Do they really wish to die alone? Why does this often happen?

Nothing is more heart-wrenching than to sit at your loved one's bedside, watching them die. Could that be the reason many choose to die alone, when the loved one momentarily steps away? Are they already seeing from the other side of the veil and know when they are alone; that it's preferable not to have the survivor see them take their last breath? Do they try to spare us?

With those thoughts, I realize that Ron came to me tenaciously in my dream at 3:00 in the morning and it woke me with a start.

. . .

That was his way of showing love for me and saying goodbye.

From an unencumbered vantage point in Spirit, did he know I would not come right away? Was he able to foresee the hour I was to return to him? Did he choose to pass away at the moment I was readying to go to him, so that he could die alone – like those who pass away the moment their loved one steps from the room? Did he know the hour I'd arrive? Did he not want me there? Once I was with him, his spirit hung in the room with all those entities. He watched me say my goodbye. He felt every bit of it. He knew how much I loved him. (I discuss this occurrence in the chapter titled *Motivations*.)

How much does the person teetering between life and death comprehend of what's left of their earthly existence? Why do they choose to pass when the people who care most have stepped away for a few moments? Is there a possibility that they have enough mindfulness and feel embarrassed about the process of leaving, or how they exit the body and, as such, wish to do it alone? It's a mystery.

(The resolution to my not being able to hold Ron at his passing is presented in the chapter titled *A Major Epiphany*.)

The following is a eulogy written by my son. When published as a particular example of writing on my former website, many people asked if they might use it in a funeral speech for their loved ones. Like then, my son gives full permission for its use; it can be changed to suit a particular person and need.

BE STRONG OF HEART

by Dean Alan (Dino) Deal

... and compassionate soul. Armor yourself against the rapacious fates but do not distress yourself with phantoms of dread. Be wise, thoughtful, and strong in the face of adversity, for no fruitless counsel can stem the flow or alter the progress of time.

The wounds perpetrated upon your spirit are not mortal; they are but enlightenment, timely stops on the path that each of us travel. These afflictions upon our joy are the necessary balance against unrestrained hedonism. Within these counterpoints of life are found pearls of wisdom and the lasting meanings of life well spent.

We do not smile or rejoice at the visage of death, but neither do we skulk away in fear or seek countless avenues of oblivion. We stand our ground and measure our success against the life well led by those who are no longer with us, knowing full well our time will eventually come, and many may learn from our life.

Upon the passing of those well beloved, we must not meander in sadness and grief. In the summation of their lives, we must ask ourselves: have we acquitted ourselves as well? Will we make them proud for the gifts they have sought to bestow upon us? It is within our grasp to give even greater meaning to their lives by incorporating within us all that they gave.

Within the cycle of life and death, we continue within those we touch, and commend the future of humankind.

30
A NEIGHBOR WHO CARES

Rita Mitchell, a neighbor across the driveway, has been a comfort to me every time we speak. She knows how I grieve for Ron and is sympathetic and never patronizing. Here she talks about her own periods of dealing with death and how she handled what life dealt her.

RITA MITCHELL: HIDDEN GRIEF

My friend and neighbor, Mary Deal, asked me to write something about grief for her book – something from my personal experience. My first response to Mary was, "Well, I don't think I've really experienced true grief. I'm not sure I would be able to add anything that would be helpful." With the very recent passing of Mary's Ron, I have been thinking about how I would (how I could) handle it if my only husband of 49 years passes away before I do.

That notion became very real for me over the last month when my husband, Rick was hospitalized with congestive heart failure and kidney failure. For the first time, I've been thinking about what it would be like for me to go through what Mary is going through now. How would I handle it?

My mother, Clara, passed away from cancer about a month after my twin sister and I were born. We were born on Nov 19, 1950, and Clara passed away on that Christmas Eve. Our brother, Stephen, was 2 years old. (I can't imagine what it is like knowing that you are dying and leaving a two-year-old son and newborn twin daughters.) I remember people asking me as a child, and even in my young adulthood, "Do you miss your mother?"

I didn't understand why people would ask me that because I never knew my mother; how can you miss someone you never knew? We had a loving, live-in housekeeper that took care of us children until my father remarried when my twin sister and I were three and our brother was five.

When Rick's mother passed, it was very sad for all of us in Rick's family. But they were very old, in ill health, and it was a natural thing that they would pass away. It was sad to lose them. I miss them. I didn't think of losing them as a grieving process. The same for my father, who was mostly absent during my childhood—i.e., *working late* because he didn't want to come home to his shrew of a second wife. Dad was happy around Rick and I and Annie, our daughter, but we didn't have the type of relationship that would lead to prolonged grief after he passed away from a stroke at an old age.

When Mary asked me to contribute as we stood outside our homes talking on a beautiful day, I said I didn't think I could. When Mary then asked me one or two leading questions, I started to tear-up and cry. I realized that I did have a story about grieving that I could share. I think I've tamped it down over the years. That, in itself, is a story about one way to handle grief, or how I handled the grief of losing my seven-year-old niece, Claire, my twin's daughter.

Claire was born before I was married to Rick and before I had my own daughter. I was a devoted aunt to Claire and I still am to her older brother, Benjamin. I took them on weekends, sleepovers at Aunt Rita's apartment, swimming, movies, roller-skating. Pampered them on their birthdays, Christmas, and all year round. Claire was a truly special person, a beautiful little girl with wisdom well beyond her age. Claire died from a congenital disease: Cystic Fibrosis. She was diagnosed at three months and passed away at age seven.

When Claire passed away, my sister and I were with her in her hospital room. I remember sitting at the head of Claire's bed, putting my arms around her shoulders. I knew the second she had passed. I felt her presence just above us and she stayed with us for a good while. She was trying to make it easier for us.

My sister and I cried, of course, and held each other. We didn't lose faith because, in her short life, Claire taught us by example to, at all times, have faith and always face hardship and adversity. I felt Claire's comfort as her spirit stayed with us. Then, I felt helpless that there was nothing I could ever do to ease this loss for my sister.

In the years after Claire passed, I did not handle my sister's grief very well. She grieved endlessly and still does. I thought that ignoring it and just moving on, not putting yourself and all the people around you through the endless pain and sadness was the better thing to do. But her constant bringing up of Claire during every moment of her life, her other children's lives, and in the lives of everyone around her made me wish that she would deal with it differently.

I didn't realize that bringing Claire up all the time wasn't just depressing, it was a way of sharing the happy times with Claire and having Claire's spirit live on. I have learned to be more open to having dialogue about Claire with my sister, and realize that talking about Claire doesn't have to bring up only pain and sorrow, but also all the joy that Claire meant to us. The more I have been open to that, the easier it is for my sister and for me.

I think I've tried to avoid grief as much as possible during my life. I've tried to not burden or sadden anyone else with my grief for fear of making them sad. By knowing Mary and being friends with her, I think I am learning things from her that will help me deal with the grief I've hidden away over the years and prepare me for facing grief in the future. I think we were put together here in our little Scottsdale community for a reason.

Indifference

The universe is indifferent
Life on earth can be cruel
and love hurts
when felt through grief

31

DWELLING ON
MEMORIES

One of the facial expressions I'll always remember is when Ron set out to do something; chin slightly thrust forward, with a look of wanting to know what lay ahead. With determination, he'd seem ready to go after whatever he had to face; good, bad, or indifferent. Time and again, I saw this same determined look of both hope and helplessness on his face as he dealt inwardly with his illness. However, the facial gestures did not represent his illness; they represent his overall attitude toward life with both its elation and vagaries. I've caught many of his images in photographs during our years together. They speak to me. I will cherish them forever.

Unbalanced

Your sweet face
full of doubtful hope
weighing on you
like scales of balance
Positive thoughts
on one side
tenuously holding on
The other side
draining that strength
turning goodness to ruin
defeating balance
tipping you away
forever.

32

WHEN DOES IT END?

At one point I felt crying was too hard and taking place for too long. A few days short of two months of Ron being gone, through tears, I asked out loud, "When does it end?" I felt crying had to stop.

In recent days, crying seemed annoying, even selfish. If Ron was *up there* somewhere watching me suffer, he wouldn't want that. He would want me to move on like we planned. Yet, when I think about him being gone forever, more tears flow. I could only hope if he were watching, he knows my tears come from my love for him, because that's what I feel when I cry . . . that I have all this love to give him and must hold it back inside my heart.

Crying is not a sign of weakness or trying to exaggerate feelings of grief. It's simply an outpouring from the cycle of sorrow, as if grief has a mind of its own. The treadmill of its cycle will eventually run its course. I know this now because when I determine not to cry and be unhappy, I can be doing anything else and feelings of grief will roll through my nervous system, cause my throat to constrict, and I will start crying, seemingly for no reason. It's like something my mind and body are trying to purge or control but will take much effort to calm. Still, I go on working through my days.

This is all part of grief's pattern and, in the future, it will subside. I know this because of my cherished widow and widower friends who stand by me, offering comfort despite my grief opening their own wounds. These special friends have gone on to build lives without their beloved partners. I am making a great effort to move on as well. Yet, I am still in the throes of accepting that Ron is gone forever, and haven't quite accepted it. The hope I hold comes from knowing my friends have built new lives and that I will be able to do that as well, yet, never ever forgetting my Ronnie.

The Ghost of You

The house is eerily quiet
too quiet
since you left
I jump at each new noise
hoping to attribute all
to the ghost of you
not wanting to leave this place
I wake in the middle of the night
to a strange but innocuous sound
I lay quietly
wondering and praying
that each new
creak, rustle, or swish
is you not wanting to leave me
I can only hope
that you will be with me
in some manner and way
forever
even as you've taken on
a new form of being
with the Angels.

33

A JOURNAL ENTRY

May 26, 2021, one day short of two months after Ron's passing. I woke in the morning mentally singing this verse. It's the same rhythm of Frank Sinatra's, *Among My Souvenirs*, but my mind has kicked out my own lyrics.

There's nothing left for me
of life that used to be
only a broken heart
among my memories

I still cry, even weep sometimes when grief uninvitedly sweeps through my nervous system. However, I realize this verse was a message to myself that I know what I have left: a broken heart and memories. As long as the memories include Ron, maybe that will help piece back together these shattered dreams.

"Dear lovely Death
That taketh all things under wing
Never to kill
Only to change
Into some other thing
This suffering flesh,
To make it either more or less,
But not again the same
Dear lovely Death,
Change is thy other name."

— LANGSTON HUGHES

The Essence of Us

The essence of us runs through this home
The furniture we chose
our style preferences blending
The kitchen we shared
till you became the better cook
The noises we made
laughter or soul soothing silence
The clothes we chose to wear
dressing for one another
The personal time we needed alone
never depriving each other
The means of recreation
golf, hiking or huffing at the gym
Our home the hub of our lives

The essence of us once ran through this house
Expensive furniture being sold
to people of varying preferences
No pots and pans rattling
I rarely cook and eat out more
This house is mostly silent
except for keyboard clicks
Your closet is now empty
your fine clothes useful to many
I have time on my hands
facing this loneliness without you
My present recreation is packing
deciding what to keep or discard
Our home was once the hub of our lives

Our essence barely present in this empty
    house
Fragments of lives well-lived

dispensed in many directions
The air is still as I walk the empty rooms
hearing echoes of our laughter
feeling the now soul numbing silence
that fills my every cell with grief
The only place you reside forever
inside my heart and mind
our souls inseparably entwined
together and always will be
as I close the door behind me
unable to return to a life that used to be
our home now just a memory.

34

THE NESTING URGE

The comment "Oh, you'll find someone new" is one that many survivors hear. I understand from where that belief originates. Almost every creature in life, animal, mammal, or human, embodies what's called a *nesting urge*. Individuals want to pair up, have a mate. It's inborn.

The people who make remarks of finding someone new are seeing grief from the position of the nesting urge.

Some people choose to look for a new mate right away and even marry quickly. Others eventually seek new partners, especially when a young person loses their partner. A few older people, who've had long-term unions, may also seek someone new right away, regardless of age, because they only know how to function within a relationship.

After a few months, I went to the mall looking for a better chain for the pendant I had made of Ron's thumbprint. At lunch, I sat alone due to tables being spaced per COVID pandemic regulations. As I ate, I watched families happy in their contained little worlds. I watched couples flirting and laughing. I saw no sad faces, then realized I was probably the only one sitting alone, ready to cry. I will never experience that kind of happiness again. I left immediately and broke out in tears before even making it to my car. I will never be part of a couple again. I miss Ron and feel no desire to have anyone replace him.

With the loss of Ron, and at my golden age, I no longer identify with the nesting urge. I want to live alone with my memories, which include all that he and I shared. I will admit that it took me nearly twenty years to fully understand how that man's mind worked. I wanted to know him inside and out and feel I didn't truly know the man to that intense degree until much time had passed; it was a fun adventure. If I were much younger, the nesting urge might still be active. At the age I find myself now, clearly not enough time is left to get to know anyone overly well. I wouldn't feel comfortable. I owe it to myself, and to Ron—who gave me his all—to make something more of my life and endeavors, and to live with our beautiful memories as long as I exist.

What Was it All Worth?

The things we said to one another
the things we did together
We lived our lives
through good times and bad
always hoping for the best
thankful when we got it
learned when we didn't
Then suddenly one of us
is gone
Everything that went before
is no more
What was it all worth?
We stuck by one another
like two people becoming one
helping each other through life
It's all we can do
while we are here
always wondering why
yet relying on each other
to get us through our years
making the purpose of life
to be kind
knowing we all face the same end
When friends die
especially loved ones
we need to know
we had done our best for them
that we succeeded in helping another
That is the purpose of life
because it adds meaning to existence
since we do not know why we are here.

35

AN OVERALL VIEW

One of the most difficult phases for me moving through this transition was trying to let go of the heartbreaking memories and images of Ron's last days in the hospital. This period bothers me more than all the rest. During his illness, we always had hope. The third time he went into the hospital, all that changed.

I was in denial of his dying. The nurse had told me that Ron asked how long he had left to live. My immediate reply to the nurse was, "Why would he ask that? His radiation and immunology treatments are working. We're going to get his legs strong again and resume his therapies."

I was deep in denial. The fact that Ron had asked how much time he had left was surely due to having been told he was terminal. Even as I experienced disbelief, as I saw him slipping away, I knew he didn't have long. Yet, I couldn't show negative emotion because I didn't want his last memory to be one of seeing me unhappy. I wanted him to see me positive and diligently attentive to him. It's all I had to offer.

Those last memories and images of him carry a lot of residual emotion and guilt now that he's gone.

In hindsight, now I try to learn from my experiences in order to, in some small way, help others understand.

My afterthoughts were that if we could have paid attention to his headaches, we could have caught the cancer earlier, at the first sign of him having more than one headache. Normally, he never had them. A little later, he began to have difficulty eating and swallowing, and experienced loss of appetite. Too late, I learned that the digestive system is one of the first bodily functions to start ceasing activity when a person is terminally or gravely ill.

Radiation and immunology treatments had drastically shrunk Ron's tumors. The doctors were amazed. Had we paid attention and caught his cancers earlier, before the tumors expanded, we might have been able to prolong his life a little longer, years, perhaps. Yet, the inevitable would happen now or later, and this is hindsight that can only offer knowledge to help others pay earlier and closer attention to their loved one's condition.

————

No matter how many differences you've had while your loved one was alive, while experiencing grief you will come to realize how much you've loved that person—and now you've no way to express that love and caring. You may also experience regret at having had differences, regardless whether they were legitimate. Grief can be a time to balance how we live, how we love or dislike in the future. Whether or not we go on to find a new partner, the grief phase can be a chance to examine how we treat others.

· · ·

Your grief period could leave you with a lot of love you must now hold inside your heart, or this phase in the process can overflow with regret.

If you loved your departed, do something to show thankfulness for the life they lived, even if it's simply to pray for their soul. Do something to keep the memory of them alive for as long as possible. Do something that helps you feel you're giving back to them, even as they are no longer here.

I will have a tribute corner in my new home expressly for Ron's mementos and photos. I plan to put his golf putter into a shadow box under an enlarged photo of him on the golf course holding that putter. I have other long-range public plans to keep his life and purpose alive that will benefit many others. One would be to establish the college scholarship that he had intended to do. I will not thoroughly mention all those plans here because they are in the incubation stage. For the time being, I honor Ron by writing this book to help others. He is the reason for this book, honoring the wonderful life we shared.

Helplessly

You may never know
the extent of your love
for someone
until you sit helplessly
beside them
as they lay dying.

36
WITH THE PASSAGE OF TIME

It's been over four months since Ron passed away. I'm still having counseling sessions, though not as frequent. I cry less, but when something triggers a special memory, tears spring from nowhere. I have been able to get through the grueling days of never-ending legal forms and filings because I have to.

Sometimes, I can turn off my feelings and immerse myself in the legalities and take on new problems that arise. I haven't had to hire legal assistance. Our private bankers have both been immense help and guidance. Ron and I knew how to handle our businesses. I didn't feel the need to have anyone manage what I could. However, I didn't realize how difficult it would be to do during the onslaught of grief; yet I have managed, as everyone must do with or without a financial manager.

I have friends who could not take time off and went back to work the day after their spouses died. Though we survivors are much aggrieved, some business or legalities will not let us delay for another day. We soon find that we will be able to manage these things, though our hearts are heavy and memories haunt us. Like this one.

———

According to Ron's doctors in 2007 and 2008, we knew Ron's cancer might return after ten years. Ron made it well past that time frame. Yet, he knew as he aged that his energy was waning. After sixty years of playing golf, he stopped in 2018 because his energy wouldn't hold. I saw it too.

On November 14, 2020, I thought he had a stroke because he couldn't use his legs, couldn't walk, or hold himself up. I rushed him to Emergency. The doctor said the mass in his brain could have been growing for years. Still, when cancer takes hold, it can grow fast. We had no way of knowing how long it had been present. I realized the moment the doctor showed me the images that we were in for a battle.

They whisked him away in an ambulance to a neurological hospital. I couldn't go. The COVID pandemic was raging in full force. For the rest of his week-long stay, I was allowed to be his only visitor for three hours each day. I found his attitude had changed. He seemed to keep anger and disappointment bottled inside. I knew the prognosis was serious, but the doctors offered hope with new medicines and therapies. When he was released a week later, stabilized and able to get around with a walker, he began radiology and immunology treatments. It was four grueling months of MRIs, CT scans, blood work-ups, treatments and double treatments.

Ron and I never spoke of his impending end. We also never discussed what I needed to do after he was gone. All that had been talked about long before. We had planned well, for either of us who might go first. However, we no longer had lots of time to speak. At our home, medical personnel came and went daily, as did numerous others. When Ron and I did speak, it was to advise he had no headache, or to laugh our way through his physical therapy exercises, or what we might cook for a strengthening meal. He spent a lot of time still reading, a book a day, or sleeping in his recliner with golf airing on TV.

We knew we'd stick by each other. Life had changed. We used to eat out a lot; now we cooked at home. Halfway through his illness, one morning as I prepared to start breakfast, he said, "Mary, you don't have to cook for me."

My immediate response was, "I'm never leaving you. I will do whatever it takes to get you well."

I realized he knew I was exhausted and was giving me the option of backing out of our agreement to stick together.

He had long-term insurance that would cover him if he went into a 24/7 care facility. He'd be taken care of. Evidently, he felt he needed to let me know he wouldn't hold me to my promise and wouldn't think poorly of me if I could no longer endure the stress. Yes, I *was* feeling the stress and was bone weary all the time, but no way would I stick him into a facility and give up looking after him. His telling me I didn't have to cook for him gave me the option to test myself, to be strong and endure, or to fold. I was still learning from him.

Ron got stronger. His tumors had shrunk down to

nearly half their sizes. Once in a while, he'd have a setback. His legs were always weak and he'd fall. Once, when he tumbled from his swivel rocker, I couldn't pick him up; and had to call 911. From that point on, I saw Ron begin to fail. He was a toughie though. He insisted on walking one block. While out, he fell at the other end of the block—yet he was determined to come home by himself instead of calling me. I also think, in his panic mode, he was confused about how to use his phone. He did make it home, falling into my arms at the front door with grass stains and bloodied knees. I vowed never again to let him go for walks without me.

A week later, he decided to try again. Only a few yards out the front door, I watched his steps falter. He couldn't make his legs move. Then, he collapsed. Neighbors ran to help me lift him when I brought out his wheelchair. That was his last walk.

A week after that, when his color was pallid, he said he felt weak, refused breakfast, and nearly melted out of his chair. That was the third and last time I rushed him to Emergency.

After Months

The rooms of our home
that you loved so much
The corners and niches
that you favored
The streets in our sweet community
that we were pleased to live among
The golf course where you played
still makes me choke up as I drive by
Everything reminds me of you
Even now after months of your passing
I see you everywhere
I feel you in every breath I breathe
My heart still aches
I long to escape
go somewhere that doesn't cause pain
But can I leave this place we called home
the last place you lived
the last place we shared our love
Can I leave this sacred place behind
to start the new life you wanted for me?

37

STILL LEARNING

Something that I thought a lot about after Ron was gone was: who am I now, without my partner, my rock? How do I go back to living alone? Do I go back to the same life to continue on without him?

One thing I knew for certain was that I could never return to the same person that I'd been before we met. For thirty-one years we grew together; the former me long gone.

As we discussed ages ago, Ron had wanted me to go on. He would say, "Keep going. Do more. Your creativity seems endless. Don't limit yourself." He had such faith in me.

Now, I've come to realize that I have learned from the experience of Ron's death. I continue to learn from remembering the years we spent together and from the strong determined person he was, in his quiet way, and how it helped him progress.

I recognize that I am stronger than I thought.

. . .

I will go on. I will build a new life for myself, a new life in Ron's memory, having emulated his determination and made it my own. I never knew I would be strong enough to face this time and see him through it. At times, I still fear I could cave into the deepest grief I've ever known.

Many more strengths will be revealed to me as I start a new life. Yes, I will go back to writing my books, painting my canvasses, and photographing for my online galleries. Ron, my mainstay, my editor, my constructive critic, will not be here to guide my work, but I remember all that he has taught me, and will continue to emulate his work ethic. I am elderly in years but still have the energy of a thirty-five-year-old. I look forward to starting my new life. It will be in memory of the love Ron and I shared. I hope he will always be looking over my shoulder.

A Lifetime Ago

Memories of our good times
the life we built
our travels
a loving home
beautiful possessions
trendy clothes
always studying
feeding our minds
learning more and more
about helping our world
seems a lifetime ago
Now as I relocate
to start a new existence
without you
I cherish a few mementos
I've chosen to keep
welcome reminders
of the wonderful life we lived
and loved together.

38

HOW CHANGE TAKES PLACE

We need to give ourselves time to work through our grief. Sometimes, we are so absorbed in our emotions and memories that we unintentionally neglect what is right in front of us.

Grief is a natural occurrence. It comes over us without provocation. Therefore, why pretend it doesn't exist or think we have to change the way we deal with it? The fact it is natural and not contrived is proof we need to accept it and move through the process at our own pace. It is our own unique emotional odyssey.

Grief is learning to live without your loved one.

In the fourth month of grieving, my counselor began to see a change in my poetry, from raw emotion to softening memories. Yes, I share everything with him. I express my emotions and feelings through writing. It helps him understand more about me then if I have to guess at how I am from day to day.

I no longer cry every day. Actually, I try to control much of that in public, put on a happy face when I can, and the crying is only in private when sadness overwhelms me. I still choke, feel my heart seize up each time I pass the golf course or have a meal in a restaurant that Ronnie preferred.

Sometimes, I get to a point of frustration wondering when all this sadness will end. Instead of allowing myself to feel such self-centered emotions—though they can be unavoidable—I've learned that if we simply sit quietly in the deepest moments of grief, we can *listen*. The memories will not stop playing in hurtful ways in our minds. We simply need to move mentally with the flow of our thoughts without interjecting our distress into them. That is how I experienced the magnificent breakthrough as described in the next chapter.

On Love Alone

We come into this world
on love alone
The quality
of the life we live
will be shown to us
by the dying
as they depart
on love alone.

39

A MAJOR EPIPHANY

(This is a follow up to the earlier chapter titled *At That Very Moment*.)

Today, August 27, 2021, is the five-month anniversary of Ron's passing. Each anniversary, at 6:15 am, the time that he died, I light a candle and have my meditation, his ashes with me.

Backtrack a second. If you've read my poem, *A Wounded Bird*, presented earlier in this book, you know that I am greatly bothered by the fact I had not held Ron one last time before he died. That poem was written when I thought about his very last moments, and the memory haunts me.

Today, as I slipped deep into meditation, all I could think about was how much Ronnie suffered, how quietly, how bravely. I remember the last hours I was with him at Hospice, how he suddenly choked on bodily fluids because he could no longer swallow. He choked and gagged so hard. His eyes popped open and he bolted upright in bed looking straight at me as I sat facing him. He couldn't breathe. His eyes begged for help. I quickly brought my legs up onto the bed and held our upper bodies together as I gave him comfort the only way I could—all I could do was grab hold of him and press him to me. Even near death, he struggled valiantly to breathe.

I spoke softly, reassuring him. "It's me, Ronnie. Mary. I'm here." I rubbed his back and the back of his neck. He stopped choking but moved his jaws as if chewing, trying to bring something up. I clung to him, held him to me for as long as I dared. He continued to gag.

I pushed the red button for the nurse. She arrived in seconds. Quickly, I told her what happened as I lay Ron back down, his gaze still on me. Then his eyes closed again. With small sponges, the nurse proceeded to extract copious amounts of fluids from his mouth. She had to remind him to open his mouth, which he did somewhat. Even that close to death, he evidently still heard and understood. I had to assume these fluids were part of the process of dying.

After the nurse left, he seemed to settle back into his coma. I continued gently rubbing his chest, his cheeks and forehead, his arms, and shoulders. I held his hands and entwined our fingers. All the while, I spoke softly, reminding him about our love, and about some highpoints in our life together. I sang our private little song. I stayed for hours.

(I learned later that evening from a retired nurse friend that this choking episode was the body's way of releasing fluids; yes, it is part of the dying process. She told me it happens near the end of life and that he didn't have long.)

After Ron passed away, I was always haunted by the trauma he endured. When I thought about the horror of him choking and gagging, that was all that came to mind. Now, this morning in meditation, unlike I wrote in *A Wounded Bird*, it came to me that I DID hug him one last time—while he was still alive and thrust into a lucid moment. It didn't happen close to the hour of his death the next morning, but I DID hug him one last time . . . the last time I was with him. He looked straight at me. He knew I was there, knew I held him when he choked. I felt him fold into my arms as I pulled him to me and he choked and gagged while his chin rested on my shoulder. I DID hold him and comfort him one last time!

This was a major revelation this morning. The emotional release I felt remembering the details of this episode was instantly cathartic. I could only sit with tears pouring as I gave thanks to God for the memory of *all* the details I had overlooked, and for removing the guilt that I had about not holding him so he could feel us together one last time.

A Shift

It crept up on me
as I wallowed for months
in the sadness
of how your illness ravaged you
Time and again
I relived the tragedy
that stole you from me
You are always on my mind
with other thoughts creeping in
flashes of happier moments
your goodness
your long life
your successes
your wit and sense of humor
Quite surprised
I feel a shift
Though my grief may never end
suddenly it's taken on
a different quality
Even as I remember
all you've accomplished
happier phases of our lives
the love we shared
I still feel unquenchable sadness
over your absence
Yet there was much more to you
then just the gravity of your death
it's how you lived
that's most important
the selfless person you were
is what I will remember most.

40

HELPING
FAMILY COPE

Another reason for immediately writing this book from *inside* my grief is because we never know when illness and impending death may visit any of us.

My brother, Charley, lives in California and is unable to visit me in Arizona. He was both on the phone and also constantly texting his support for me during the entire time Ron was ill and particularly after Ron passed away. To this day, my brother supports me. However, as I wrote earlier, his wife was also ill.

Charley's wife, Dottie, was being treated for brain and breast cancer for more than a year before my Ron was diagnosed. Dottie's surgery and treatments were also working for her and she was improving more than remarkably. Yet, somewhere while I was busy caring for Ron, Dottie's condition went downhill. She died August 16, 2021. Now it is I who support my brother, the same way he cared about my wellbeing.

No one can predict anything like this. It is fate playing its cruelest hand.

· · ·

The only solution to what life deals us is to FOCUS on the challenge of the moment and manage the issues as best we know how at that point in time. Now, I forget about my grief and woes and focus on helping my brother deal with emotions like those I know all too well and still experience.

Likewise, I hope this book helps others living through their loved one's demise and the unpredictable grief process that starts the moment we face their terminal prognosis. The cliché, *one day at a time,* is how we focus and help ourselves move through this heart-wrenching period.

Never Once

You fought hard
the greatest battle of your life
never once complaining
never heard you
make negative comments
about anything
the many years
we've been together
Never once
negativity
that might tear
at our equilibrium
You remained positive
enduring
all those treatments
medical insults to the body
against graver insults of illness
that won
The strong and the weak
moments and days
weeks and months
right to the end
never once
a negative or fearful comment
leaving behind
the beauty of your countenance
a lesson that never once
are negative comments
nor complaining
necessary or productive.

41

WHAT I BELIEVE

It's my belief that when we transition into the Afterlife, we become free of all elements of our earthly cares and woes. In that sense, we should not fear again meeting those with whom we shared an earthly life, regardless if it was good, bad, or indifferent. This physical existence keeps us captive. Yet, when it's our turn to meet those departed on the other side, all worldly matters will be left behind. We are never affected by them again. Yet, we are wiser souls.

Our departed ones are pure souls, knowing only love and peace, and that is what we'll find when we meet them again. It will be all we, too, become when it's our turn to cross over. I've believed this all my life. It sustains me. I can't wait to meet my loved ones on the other side, to know them in their pure soul essences, devoid of all worldly influence.

———

I urge others to pay attention to what's happening in their thoughts. Sit quietly once in a while and simply listen to what goes on in your mind. Many thoughts will come and go. Some will spark deep interest and hold your attention. Sometimes, when we give our minds a rest, messages can come through and in dreams too. Whether or not you practice meditation, simply sitting quietly is a great technique for centering yourself and getting a grip on all those rampant thoughts that keep causing pain.

Some of my experiences with centering in my quieter moments follow:

1. Several times over the years since my ex-husband (my son's father) passed away, he has come to me in dreams and thoughts. Each time he appears, I learn that he comes to collect a family member; he always appears before a family member dies. I receive more details about each situation that confirms what I believe, but that much is not pertinent here.

2. My dad came to me, first in thought, for about two months during the summer of 2015. The way I identified my dad was that I could hear and repeat his Filipino language, even the cuss words. It filled my mind. Then, on August 11, 2015, while standing quietly at my computer, wondering what work to tackle next, I felt a Spirit behind me. It came up close, touched both my upper arms and leaned forward, as if placing its chin on my shoulder. My dad actually did that! When I was younger, he would come up behind me, grab both my upper arms, rest his chin on my shoulder and look to see what I might be reading or writing.

By then, I was able to see all around me without turning my head. What a feeling! I knew that if my dad came that close, it could be my time to pass away. Strangely, I had no fear. I turned my head toward my left shoulder where I felt him, and said, "Well, hi!" I really didn't know what else to say. I was surprised and in a bit of awe. Without knowing if I were to die soon, I went about my business, trying to wrap up anything important as Ron and I had long ago planned, though I didn't tell Ron about my dad right away. I lived the next few months, wondering—given I was in such good health—how was I going to die?

During the week after Christmas, I had five or six visitations. I felt a Spirit appear behind me, first on one side, then another. Again, I saw the area behind me without turning my head. Each time it appeared, I perceived a feeling of deep curiosity from the visiting Spirit. I knew it wasn't my dad, but thinking of my dad's visit, I wondered if some of his distant family might be passing. Not until January 17, 2016 did I hear that my sister, whom no one had seen for about fifty years, had passed away on December 26, 2015. I realize that she had most likely been the Spirit that visited me after Christmas, before I learned she was gone. Many say the departed will spend some time visiting family and others before moving on.

3. My dad (and his language) came again several times before and after Ron fell ill. Dad was not a strong entity those times. Still, I wondered about me. After Ron was diagnosed, I realized it was my dad supporting me.

4. Often in the last five and one-half months since Ron died, I began to sing the old songs my mother sang to my siblings and me. Mom died in 1996. Ron reciprocated by staying close and taking away my cares and interruptions. We were living on Kauai then and he planned the immediate trip back to the mainland. One way I remember mom is with her singing, hearing it from my infancy. She and all her family were musicians and singers. Recently, it wasn't until this second time that I caught myself singing (singing

during grief?) that I remembered something that had stayed with me. After my dad died, mom always sang the song, *Have I Told You Lately That I love You?* I have heard it in my head many times over the last few months. It's my belief that my mother is sending a message that she understands my predicament because of her own loss. That song is our connection. It's my mom supporting me from Spirit.

NOTE: *Have I Told You Lately that I Love You?* written by Scotty Wiseman for the 1944 musical film, *Sing, Neighbor, Sing,* and performed by him and his wife, Lulu Belle.

Though I could quote many instances of messages from loved ones in Spirit, I will give just one more . . . this one most important.

5. Ron never particularly delved into things of the Spirit. Yet, a few months after his eldest sister died in 2019, he told me of a dream (and he usually never remembers his dreams). He dreamed he saw his mother, dad, step-dad, and sister sitting at a table in Heaven. He saw one empty chair. Ron woke feeling that empty chair was meant for him, like a premonition revealing that his time was close.

Doubtful Hope

Your weakened
and frail body
your sweet face
full of doubtful hope
endures in my memory
forever.

It is said that we survivors most remember the last few days of our departed loved one. I find this to be true. While we care for our loved ones during their illness, it's those last crucial days—when they may be filled with questionable hope concerning their longevity—that we remember most.

Ron's expression always seemed positive in a struggling sort of way, always with that look as if saying: *this is what's happening now. I'll do my best.* Though weakness progressed daily, his attitude and willingness to do whatever it took said he would meet head-on whatever was dealt him. I can't help thinking that inside he was also scared of the unknown that was about to claim him. I knew him well. I'd catch him with a pensive or distant stare and he'd smile that special way again when he caught me studying him.

Months earlier, before his first radiation treatment, I had asked if he was nervous about such grave treatments. His hesitation to reply said he held a lot of trepidation. After the treatment, I asked again. He admitted he had been fearful, only because he didn't know what to expect, but that it had been "a piece of cake!" My greatest hope was that because radiation was easy for him, the unknown no longer frightful, that he accepted passing away without fear. Yes, the brain bleed did claim him quietly, but during his last cognitive thoughts, I hope his fright of the unknown had somehow been eased. I felt his level of anticipation, felt him acknowledging that nothing more could be done to alleviate pain or fear, nor his dying. I felt his acceptance of it all.

Those last days and moments will haunt us the most and will take time to soften. We need to remind ourselves to think of better times. Surely, we've experienced lots of happiness and those moments are how we should remember our loved ones. We will always remember the struggle during their last days, but those images should take their places amid the more joyful times.

I had occasion to have an x-ray at the same lab where I took Ron time and again. One long ramp was available for those who could not climb the stairs to the entrance. When we were there the last time and ready to leave, it rained profusely. One benevolent lady saw Ron and me struggling in the downpour. She offered to hold her umbrella over Ron's head while he eased his walker down the slope. I walked backwards, in front of him, to assure he nor his walker slipped. All three of us got drenched.

Today, in bright sunlight, I walked the ramp instead of the stairs and snapped pictures of it and quietly said, "Ronnie, this is for you." I knew my sorrows were easing. I could look at that ramp and sadly relive the memory of us struggling together, but . . . I did not cry.

$$42$$

ADJUSTING

I t is strange not having to allot my time to fit Ron's medical schedules or to be ready in case of another emergency. I had stopped working all together. Now, the transition back to work feels like entering a foreign country. Life's matrix has shifted.

Life offers great beauty
while death offers tragedy
to balance our souls.

Maybe the reason Ron went peacefully was because he knew dying was inevitable, especially with his illness ravaging his brain functions. Maybe he reflected on our life together while his mind was still active, though he couldn't speak and was slipping away—remembering us, a way to feel his life was worthy. Maybe he held my face in his mind, the face he always watched, then shared his loving grin. Maybe he found courage in that, making it easy to accept the inevitable as I watched him fade away.

After months, as I face the workload of my usual days, even as I prepare this manuscript, I find I am still numb. At times, my thoughts drift to many other things. Sometimes, I need distraction and get out of my chair and move around in order to return to full concentration. All of these moods I attribute to being numb. It's as if I live my days on a slightly different plain, not yet having quite the same zeal for the work that I love doing. What is most difficult to deal with: certain dismal memories that keep repeating and re-peating until I think I'll go mad.

————

Now, nearly six months after Ron's passing, I feel my energy gathering again. I've handled an extreme amount of paperwork and don't know how I did it, except that in the back of my mind, I kept thinking: ***this is what we prepared each other for.***

A couple weeks ago, I managed to laugh for the first time in many months. My counselor says I am con-quering my grief faster than most because I face it head-on. Many people refuse to acknowledge their grief. They need to know that it will always be present and needs to be addressed before it can truly ease. I am getting on with my life and taking Ron with me. If anything, what writing this book has taught me is that Ron wanted me to have a good life . . . till we meet again.

My counselor advises that I write letters to our departed loved ones. Today, I have well over two hun-dred pages of letters and notes I've written to Ron. I am fast on the keyboard, and talk to him as if he were here. It gives me a chance to organize my days and to let him know special events that are happening. Writing is an amazing tool to work through the problems that accompany this stage in life. Writing keeps him in my life.

———

Lately, when I choke up, I try to distract myself. I still cry some because I've found no better release when I become overwhelmed, like when the check came from his life insurance. I held it in my hands, trembling all over. To think he had to die for me to receive this. I began to cry again, bawling like a soul lost with no means of return. This is a gift from my Ron, who keeps on giving, and I have no way to thank him except to write letters and speak my thoughts and feelings to his picture, and write this book intended to help others, a gift from Ron who keeps on giving.

Full Circle

Love originating before time
doesn't come to full fruition
till one of the partners
leaves with the Angels
Life can be glorious
or problem-ridden
but as long as two
remain in love
and understanding,
it isn't until one has left
that they are reminded
of the total spectrum of that love
as one endures bereavement
because grief is a measure
of their commitment.
The other who has passed
most assuredly looks down,
recognizes the heartfelt depth
of their love.
They see all, unencumbered
by human limitations.
They understand the grief
and stay near the one who lives on
guiding, sending subtle messages
knowing both will be
reunited soon enough
to bring their love
full circle.

43

SOME LAST WORDS

Today, September 27, 2021, marks six months since Ron's passing. During this period, I have experienced emotional devastation the likes I've never known. Little did I notice how, after the first three to four months, that my mental equilibrium was shifting. It was like timidly emerging out of darkness, not knowing what I would find, knowing I had to face a new me.

After enduring this most critical time in my life, I realize I have found new strength, as if I had to be taught. I learned well. I'm not totally out of the crying stage. My lifetime of cherished photographs and memories still affect me pitifully. Having faced reality head-on, I am able to go on with my life, though I still cannot fathom how I made it through all the legalities and paperwork that I had to manage (and have more to finish). Major changes coming for me: a move across the country to live near my son. I feel strong enough to handle almost anything, in memory of my Ronnie.

I could not have made it through these months without the in-depth advice and nudging of my wise and intuitive counselor, and the help of true friends who never quit caring. I am blessed.

———

(After having edited and polished the manuscript for this book, I returned to add a note from which I believe all survivors will benefit.)

On October 27th, 2021, at 6:15 in the morning, the seven-month anniversary of Ron leaving, I sat quietly with his ashes. My thoughts focused on telling him I was doing my best to get through my grief, especially fueled by the fact I had not been with him during his last moments. I needed to somehow ease that residual torment to be able to focus on the memories of our extraordinary life together. My thoughts were:

Ron is in Heaven with the Angels. The cares and woes of earthly existence no longer trouble him. He now knows only pure love and peace. He tries to show that to me with his visitations.

Like a wave that washed over me, I realized that if Ron is no longer troubled by earthly woes, no longer distressed with the same worries I carry, then why should I hang onto my regrets and let them fuel my grief? Surely, Ron does not want me to spend the rest of my life in a perpetual state of bereavement. Ron is no longer troubled by any of the sadness, mistakes and shortcomings of worldly matters. If this no longer bothers him, then neither will I allow these worries to take over me. I will live in love and memory of my Ronnie and be thankful for our soulful connection, made possible only when I allow love to rein and abolish negative thoughts and regrets. I am still learning from him.

. . . on earth as it is in Heaven.

— FROM *THE LORD'S PRAYER*

For Ron Holte

I will hold you in my heart
   to keep you alive
   like one soul that we are
   merged for all of time.

— MARY DEAL

RONALD JEROME HOLTE: OBITUARY

In Loving Memory

Ronald Jerome Holte
6/22/1934 to 3/27/2021

Ronald Jerome Holte, age 86, Scottsdale, AZ, passed away March 27, 2021, after a long battle with cancer.

Born June 22, 1934 during the Great Depression in Ulen, MN, to loving parents Carl and Thelma Tiedje Holte, children of immigrants from Norway and Northern Europe. His family moved to San Francisco, CA, at the start of WWII, residing in the Haight-Ashbury district. He attended San Francisco schools, McKinley Grammar School, Everett Jr. High, and Commerce High School, graduating 1952.

In June 1952, he started work as a locomotive fireman, on oil-burning steam engines, for Southern Pacific Railroad Coast Division between San Francisco and Santa Barbara. Ron was drafted into the US Army Signal Corp in 1957, serving on active duty twice with an Honorable Discharge. Returning to work, he chose a regular locomotive afternoon shift while entering morning classes at San Francisco Golden Gate University, a private business and law school on Golden Gate Avenue. Graduating with a Bachelor of Science in Accounting in 1962, he then resigned Southern Pacific and joined the General Accountability Office (GAO) as an Auditor, then later as a Supervisory Auditor of audit teams, serving on national and international audits until 1969.

Ron was accepted into the Master's program at CSU-Sacramento, graduating with a Master of Business Administration in 1972. While attending the Master's program, he applied for a registered stockbroker license, which was kept current until his full retirement in 2017.

Also, in 1972 he started with a large state agency where he served as Audit Manager. In addition to his day job, he started a part-time business performing taxes, small business accounting, and financial consulting. Further, he started an outsourcing corporation for small non-profit professional associations providing accounting, executive board administration, and conference and board meeting arrangements.

When starting as an entry-level auditor, he did not feel productive due to existing audit guidance. To improve productivity for auditors and audit agencies, he wrote a paper on operational audit guidance. He was invited to present the paper at the *Institute of Internal Audit International Conference* in Israel. Being well received, Ron later published the paper as an eBook on Smashwords.

In 1995, he sold his many business activities in California and moved to Kauai, HI, to play golf at Wailua Golf Course, also joining the Wednesday Club. He continued working as a financial consultant on Kauai until 2014, then downsized and purchased a condominium in Honolulu.

In 2017, he moved to Scottsdale, AZ, purchasing a patio home at McCormick Ranch, and joining the McCormick Ranch Golf Club playing till health interfered. Finally, fully retiring in 2018, he completed a long productive life that began at age twelve as a part-time grocery store clerk after school.

Ron was baptized Lutheran at birth, had no children, and was married and divorced twice. He is survived by a sister, Bonnie Wash of Rohnert Park, CA, and two nieces, Kathleen Ortiz and Erica Markham Stroud in Washington. He was pre-deceased in death by his father, Carl Holte, mother Thelma Tiedje Wilbert, and step-father Joseph Wilbert, all of San Jose, CA., and sister Sandy Ortiz of Sequim, WA. His loving partner of 31 years, Mary Deal in Scottsdale, continues hers and Ron's legacy as an author, artist, and photographer, doing business worldwide. Mary will bring Ron's ashes back to Kauai.

SPECIAL NOTE: Additionally, as the accountant for various charities, in one, a shelter established for abused women and children, Ron was the elected Treasurer. After his two-year tenure, he had managed to build the organization's meager funds to over $200K, which allowed them to finally build their women's and children's center. Another activity as a life-long golfer includes three hole-in-ones at three different golf courses. He was also an author/editor and world traveler. He was so much more and an obituary can't possibly hold all that this man accomplished and contributed to life.

ACKNOWLEDGMENTS

First, I wish to give a heartfelt thank you and express deep appreciation to my counselor, who wishes to remain anonymous. What he does to help others comes from a place of pure integrity and he accepts no remuneration from those fortunate to have his guidance. Without his expertise in managing grief in others, I most likely would have caved in and become lost in my sorrows. It's because of his guidance that I now understand the process of my grief and am getting through it. It's because of his guidance that I now more fully understand the process of living and dying.

My counselor was available for me immediately from the moment I knew Ron would pass—there for me when I realized we'd receive no miracle, through my deepest moments of sorrow, to taking me through the bereavement process with understanding and encouragement. He was totally selfless, preferring to concentrate on getting me to a better place emotionally than to bring attention to himself. He is a person who truly understands his purpose in it all. I would suggest anyone experiencing grief to seek counseling. At a time in our lives when we are numbed, another wise person will serve as the beacon that guides us.

He taught me that grief is not something we can force to stay away. Though it may be predominant in the weeks and months following our loved one's passing, it will lessen in intensity and duration. Yet it seems to come and go with life's activities and circumstances. It's like the psyche purging trauma every opportunity it finds. That is why we must allow it to happen and move through it, hopefully with the aid of a professional counselor. The trauma of grief will lessen and lessen until it reaches a manageable stage. By then, the suffering will have become different, no longer hurting, despite the sad memories that remain.

Anything I have learned about managing my grief that I pass on to readers, I learned from my counselor. It is true that my counselor advising me through my turmoil enabled me to write this book for others enduring the often-times bewildering passage through sorrow.

UNENDING THANKS

More heartfelt thanks to each and every one online and through the mails who sent prayers, sympathy and condolences. It keeps my spirits up. Also, a debt of gratitude to those who visited regularly and got me out of the house. Grief is a hard road to travel. We all do it differently, but one thing is certain: everyone's grief is unlike anyone else's. Your grief will be your very own. Caring friends and relatives help to greatly ease the heartache.

On Your Own

Working through grief
with supportive friends
is akin to having people
hold you up on both sides

But you are the one
who decides whether or not
and when
you stand on your own.

MY SUPPORT CIRCLE

My only immediate family is my son on the east coast and my brother on the west coast. My son was unable to fly here to Arizona due to the COVID pandemic. My brother, as mentioned earlier, was caregiver for his wife, who also battled brain cancer.

Having no immediate relatives close by, I wish to acknowledge the following people for standing by and helping me in so many ways. Some, among these two lists, include three of Ron's former golf partners when we all lived on Kauai. First, a heartfelt thanks to those for their contributions to this book.

Dean Alan Deal (son), Raleigh, NC
Linda Watson, Indian Wells, CA
Fran Loando, Scottsdale, AZ
Rita Vacca, Scottsdale, AZ
Susan Yamamoto, Kapa`a, Kauai, HI
Sam Woollard, Sr., Devon, UK
Rita Mitchell, Scottsdale, AZ
Sherry Rentschler, Mint Hill, NC
Christina Hanson Pierzchalski, Scottsdale, AZ

Many others helped keep my emotions on track and were supportive in my darkest moments, and kept in touch from afar, or immediately assisted me in various ways. Upon preparing this list, I realize I have been truly blessed with family and friends.

Charley Ramirez (brother), Somerset, CA
Bonnie Wash (Ron's sister), Rohnert Park, CA
Allison & Joe Tiedje (Ron's cousin), Queen Creek, AZ
Fran Loando & Charlie Rogers, Scottsdale, AZ
Christina & Tony Pierzchalski, Scottsdale, AZ
Larry Blow, Upper Black Eddy, PA
Harold Okahara, Las Vegas, NV
Christina M. Berry, Honolulu, HI
Abe Lee, Honolulu, HI
Sue Midlock-Eddy, Joliet, IL
Brenda Vidinha, Kapa`a, Kauai, HI
Julie Anne Black Caspillo, Kapa`a, Kauai, HI
Holly & Rick Schunk, Kapa`a, Kauai, HI
Susan & Doyle Whitfield, Dudley, NC
Kathryn Jones, South Shields, UK
A.J. Griffiths-Jones, Akbuk, Turkey

Melanie Gotcher, Social Worker, set us up with all the services Ron would need. Among them: Sue Hyland, nurse, and Charlynn Polacek, physical therapist. These three professionals diligently came to our home for every appointment during the COVID pandemic. Another is Joanna Dewey at *Neptune Society*, who has unending patience and understanding.

It goes without saying that the numerous doctors and medical personnel who took care of Ron—seemingly an unending list—deserve my heartfelt gratitude. These people were some of the most learned professionals I've encountered.

Mentioning everyone is impossible. Many people tried to help in any way they could, if only texting messages of support. Some have diligently kept up promotions for my books and art when I abandoned my work. As can be guessed, many were involved. If I don't mention others here, the omission is not intentional. All offers of help and support will never be forgotten. I couldn't have gotten through this most critical event in my life without all this support from both near and far.

TO MY READERS

Thank you for reading *Grief Is Love*. If my experiences help you, or if you simply enjoyed reading this memoir, it would be greatly appreciated if you would return to the site where you purchased this book and leave a review. It doesn't have to be lengthy. A short statement is enough. An author's success is built by reader reviews.

Reviews help to sell books and I want to sell enough to have a good amount of profit to donate to the ***American Cancer Society – Renal Research.***

A Suggestion:

For those who wish to learn more about the ability to sit quietly and sort out their thoughts, please read my bestselling, award-winning book titled *Hypno-Scripts: Life-Changing Techniques Using Self-Hypnosis and Mediation.*

ABOUT MY PUBLISHER

I owe a world of thanks to **Miika Hannila** and the team at **Next Chapter** publishing for doing their share, as usual, in keeping my books alive during the time I could not promote.

Here then are my books with Next Chapter, along with a brief synopsis of each.

<u>Legacy of the Tropics</u> – A trilogy of stories that shatter the myths of stereotypical islands of paradise. In **Promises**, during the late 1960s, a ketch, *Mercy*, sinks during a sea storm off Culebra near the Virgin Islands. Ciara Malloy assumes custody of her drowned fiancé's son and learns a devastating secret about the boy that changes her life forever. In **Adrift**, in the late 1990s, underwater photographer Lillian Avery gets caught in a rip current and is swept out to sea off Kauai in Hawaii. In facing death, she finds a way to leave a message behind. Years later, in **Reunion**, the two former neighbors from Puerto Rico reunite on Kauai. A hurricane wreaks island-wide havoc. Ciara is missing, presumed dead. Among the rubble, Lillian finds Ciara's memoirs, a life history that threatens to expose tightly held secrets about the boy since the sinking of the *Mercy*.

The Ka – Archaeology student Chione has vivid dreams about the discovery of an opulent tomb. After the founder of the Institute of Archaeology learns that Chione's dreams might be connected to events in Egypt, he accepts an offer to examine a mysterious site in Valley of the Queens.

When they discover a burial chamber, ancient spells transport Chione and her ex-boyfriend, archaeologist Aaron Ashby, 3,500 years into the past. There, they learn of Tutankhamun and Tauret, a priestess in Pharaoh's Court. Soon, Chione and Aaron discover that they have been chosen to play a crucial part in Tauret's seductive plan.

River Bones – Sara Mason Mysteries Book One – A serial killer is on the loose in the Sacramento River Delta. When Sara Mason returns to her hometown to start a new life, she learns that a murderer is terrorizing its residents. Despite battling difficult childhood memories, Sara is determined to make peace with her past.

She soon learns that the elusive psychopath is now stalking her. Sara's attempt to rebuild her life is hindered even more by the discovery of skeletal remains on her property. As the investigation focuses on several suspects, Sara discovers critical clues and bravely volunteers to be a decoy for the sheriff's department. Sara's destiny has brought her back home, but will her decision lead her down a path lined with danger . . . and straight into the arms of a madman?

The Howling Cliffs – Sara Mason Mysteries Book Two – Sara Mason joins her love interest, Huxley, in searching for his MIA brother's remains in the Vietnam jungle. She is joined by her friend Esmerelda. Later in Hawaii, Sara learns that a six-year-old neighborhood girl had gone missing ten years earlier. Something odd is going on at the nearby forest cliffs; someone wants this cold case to stay cold.

Even after attempts are made on Sara's life, she pushes on with the investigation and pursues the leads that take her on a path of danger. Can she solve the mystery of the Howling Cliffs?

Dead to Life – Sara Mason Mysteries Book Three – Sara Mason and Huxley Keane follow a trail of clues in an attempt to match a bullet-scarred key found in the Vietnam jungle. An apartment key was given to Rocky, Huxley's brother, by his fiancée. If sweet Emma Ellis kept a matching key all these years, it would prove Rocky is not MIA, but deceased.

Tracing Emma proves to be a perilous escapade; she doesn't wish to be found and attempts to stop Sara and Huxley, whose very lives are threatened. In separate incidences, both Sara and Huxley are left to die of their wounds. But when they finally catch her, horrifying truths about the woman send their sensibilities reeling.

Down to the Needle – From the day her five-year-old was abducted, Abigail Fisher vowed never to stop looking until her daughter was safely back home. Despite multiple searches, twenty-three years have passed without a trace of Becky Ann. When Abigail learns that death row inmate Megan Winnaker is the same age as her daughter, she begins to wonder if the kidnapper had Becky Ann's face surgically altered to prevent identification.

Megan Winnaker maintains her innocence, but faces capital punishment if she loses her final appeal. As Abigail launches her own investigation to find out if Megan is truly her daughter, someone wants to stop her in her tracks. Even when facing mortal danger, Abigail refuses to give up her investigation. But can Megan Winnaker really be her long-lost daughter?

Sea Cliff – A Love Story – Rachael Connor has great looks, money and a home of her own, but childhood abuse has left her fearful of men. When she meets Matthew, she begins to rethink her life. He falls in love with her, but Rachael rebukes him, living by the *rules* her father taught.

She soon has an epiphany about how to overcome her father's grip on her life. The next time she falls in love, she will know how to deal with it. But will Matthew let her get away so easily?

Off Center in the Attic – Humor and nonsense, flights of fantasy into other realms, fright, disgust and disappointment, silliness and wonderment, and the sadness of reality and heartache. It's all here, and more, in 30 short stories that may leave you a little *Off Center in the Attic.*

Hypno-Scripts: Life-Changing Techniques Using Self-Hypnosis and Meditation – Unleash the power of your mind and discover your potential. What are you waiting for?

Write It Right – Tips for Authors – Written and compiled by award-winning novelist Mary Deal, *Write it Right - Tips for Authors* is a major source of information for breathing life into your prose. Learn how to polish your writing with tips and examples, and make your prose leap off the page.

ABOUT THE AUTHOR

 **Mary Deal** is an award-winning and Amazon bestselling multi-genre author of suspense/thrillers, romance, a short story collection, a writers' reference, and nonfiction self-help. She is a Pushcart Prize nominee, Artist and Photographer, and former newspaper columnist and magazine editor.

Mary's first feature screenplay, *Sea Storm*, and *Chin Face*, a short story, were nominated into the Semi-Finals in a *Moondance International Film Festival* competition.

One of Mary's many short stories, *The Last Thing I Do*, appeared in the anthology, *Freckles to Wrinkles*, by *Silver Boomer Books*, and was nominated for the coveted *Pushcart Prize*.

She has traveled a great deal and has a lifetime of diverse experiences, all of which remain as fodder for her fiction. A native of California's Sacramento River Delta, where she set some of her stories, she has also lived in England, the Caribbean, the Hawaiian Islands, and now resides in Scottsdale, Arizona. In addition to originals and art prints, her paintings and photography are also used to create gorgeous personal and household products from her galleries.

To learn more about Mary Deal and discover more Next Chapter authors, visit our website at www.nextchapter.pub.

Find Her Online
Her Website: http://www.marydeal.com
Facebook: http://www.facebook.com/mdeal
Twitter: http://twitter.com/Mary_Deal
Linked In: http://www.linkedin.com/in/marydeal
Goodreads: https://www.goodreads.com/MaryDeal
BookTown: http://booktown.ning.com/
profile/MaryDeal

Her Art Galleries
Mary Deal Fine Art:
http://www.marydealfineart.com
Island Image Gallery:
https://www.zazzle.com/mbr/238769166096897633
Pinterest:
https://www.pinterest.com/1deal

BOOKS BY MARY DEAL

Mary Deal began her writing career as a mystery novelist. Not wishing to limit herself, she has branched into several genres and then into nonfiction too. These are her books:

Fiction

The Ka, a paranormal Egyptian suspense

River Bones, Sara Mason Mysteries Book One

The Howling Cliffs, Sara Mason Mysteries Book Two

Dead to Life, Sara Mason Mysteries Book Three

Legacy of the Tropics, adventure/suspense

Down to the Needle, a thriller

Sea Cliff, a contemporary romance

Collections

Off Center in the Attic, 30 Short Stories

Nonfiction

Write It Right – Tips for Authors

Hypno-Scripts – Life-Changing Techniques Using Self-Hypnosis and Meditation

Grief is Love – A Memoir of Surviving Bereavement

Grief Is Love
ISBN: 978-4-82412-679-5
Mass Market

Published by
Next Chapter
1-60-20 Minami-Otsuka
170-0005 Toshima-Ku, Tokyo
+818035793528

14th February 2022